SEARCHING HIGH AND BELOW
by
Gill Williams

First published in the United Kingdom 2020.

A catalogue record of this book is available from the British Library.

ISBN 978-1-907463-74-7

Cover © Gill Williams
(Courtesy of Philip Lee Harvey)

Published by © Plan4 Media and Plan4 Publishing

CONTENTS

Foreword

In my life, I have been fortunate to meet world leaders, celebrities and truly wonderful people who have had a positive and significant impact on others. Gill Williams QPM *(Queen's Police Medal)* is one of those truly remarkable people.

Gill joined the Thames Valley Police as a cadet in 1978 and went on to become a police officer at a time when the police was still very much a male-dominated world. Six years into her police service, she joined the force's marine section on the river patrol unit, and, subsequently, after intensive training, she became a diver.

Gill was promoted to sergeant in 1996 and became the first woman in the UK to be responsible for an underwater search unit. Realising her unit was a great cost to the Thames Valley Police, and with cutbacks looming, Gill expanded the range of services it offered to increase its value to the force. The unit began to deal with recovery of bodies on land and received specialist training in major disaster body recovery—a skill that was soon to be called upon.

Despite her training in major disaster body recovery, nothing could have prepared Gill for what she was to experience when she deployed with other police officers to lead in the identification of thousands of bodies in Thailand after the 2004 tsunami.

In March 2007, Gill was rightly honoured for her work in Thailand. The high sheriff of Berkshire presented her with the *Thames Valley Police Shrievalty Merit Award* at a special awards lunch in front of her chief constable and her very proud father. Gill was very close to her father and was devastated when he died suddenly a few days later.

In the Queen's birthday honours list the following year, Gill was further recognised for her services to policing, including in Thailand, with a *QPM* awarded by Prince Charles at Buckingham Palace.

During her deployment in Thailand, Gill met Rotjana, a lady who appeared, day after day, at the roadside, each time with another baby or child who had been orphaned by the tsunami. Gill founded a charity called *Hands Across the Water UK,* which built and supported an orphanage in Thailand for these babies and children. She, with her typical compassion, raised money for the charity in the UK by giving sponsored talks about her experiences in Thailand and by running, walking and cycling great distances. Those children were able to enjoy a loving and secure upbringing. Some of them now work at the orphanage, which currently cares for over one hundred abandoned children. Tragically, Rotjana, who became a very close friend of Gill, passed away following a long fight with cancer in 2017. She was only 51-years-old.

In her autobiography, Gill describes her experiences and emotions very well. You can vividly imagine the scene she is describing, and her anecdotal stories help the reader to understand what she has been through.

I have pestered Gill for years—in a good way—to get her to write her autobiography. I am pleased she has. This is a remarkable story about a remarkable lady. It's absorbing, interesting and at times funny—but have a box of tissues ready!

John Casson MBE

SEARCHING HIGH AND BELOW
GILL WILLIAMS

I was seated at a large round table. The silverware and white linen—all beautifully arranged. I glanced across to my dad, he looked amazing—76 years old, pure white hair and not a wrinkle on his face. What was he on? I wanted some of it. He looked so smart, and he caught my eye and winked at me. There was so much pride in those bright blue eyes and in that moment I realized just how much all of this meant to him. I could not have wished for more and just knew that he would be reliving this occasion with his many friends in the pub in the weeks ahead. I was then called up to the front of the stage to be presented with my award.

THE BEGINNING

Even as a young child, I was always charging about, not the young lady at all—a complete and utter tomboy, forever caked in mud, cut and bruised but smiling.

My dad ran St John's Boys' Club in Marston Street, Oxford and from as early as I can remember, my summers were spent playing cricket and winters playing football. I never walked but ran everywhere and to me climbing trees, swimming in rivers, and the great outdoors was like second nature. I loved everything outdoors. My bible was *Swallows and Amazons,* and life was for living. Despite being so active, I also loved reading adventure books and art, which was my favourite subject at school.

Mr. Powell, my art teacher, really pushed me in all mediums and made me believe that I was going to art college when I finished school. I felt that because I was naturally good at art, this would be something that I could do. However, part of me also wanted to work with animals as I loved any creature, including all of my pet guinea pigs over the years, our dogs and the horses I rode.

At the age of fifteen, the school offered all of the children in my year a week's work experience. I had grown up and lived on a massive council estate in Cowley, Oxford, where quite a few of my friends had dealings with the police. When it came to what I could choose—all that remained on the list was a week at Cowley police station. What the heck, at least it would be more interesting than a bank or office somewhere. I guess that week opened my eyes and turned my life around. I realized that here was the job that would offer me adventure, challenges and opportunities to help others, work in a team and plenty of physical activity.

As soon as I was old enough, I applied to become a police cadet with the Thames Valley Police (TVP). I was interviewed by Sergeant Tony Collins, who desperately wanted me on board because I was a keen runner, and he was head of the TVP cross country section. While waiting to see if I had been accepted, Mr. Powell had started me on my A-level art course—believing I guess that he could still influence his pupil. The letter arrived confirming that I was to start my police cadet training at Sulhamstead (the training centre for TVP) on Monday 24th July 1978, a week after my 17th birthday and as it turned out a week after finishing school.

I adored Mr. Powell and was saddened to see the dismay in his face that I would not be following him. However, he did cram me through my A-level course in three months which I passed with flying colours, so all was not lost.

INITIAL CADET COURSE

I can always remember driving to the Thames Valley Police Training Centre with my mum and dad and seeing the White House for the first time. I felt that I was so lucky to be given this opportunity.

 Walking through the front door into reception, I was instantly aware of the smell—wax polish. The reception hall was impressive and still is, all wood panels with a sweeping staircase opposite the doors. The smell of the polish has stayed with me throughout my career, and each time I walk into the reception, I am immediately transported back to that very first day as a young girl cadet. My mum and dad helped me in with my cases, and we were immediately met by the smartest person in uniform I have ever seen even to this day. His uniform was immaculate. You could see reflections in his shoes, they were so highly polished, and he carried a stick tucked under his arm. In a broad Geordie accent, he announced: "Say goodbye to your mum and dad, I'm your mum and dad now." I did not have time to feel sad at leaving my mum and dad because he picked up my case and said, "Follow me," and marched off. I hugged my mum and dad and went running after him, through a door and up a steep flight of narrow stairs which led me right to the top floor of the White House where my deep-voiced Geordie officer was waiting for me outside a door.

"This is your room, choose a bed and be back down in reception in half an hour."

I walked into my room and saw that I would be sharing with three other people. The room was alcoved, dark with a small window looking out across the Berkshire countryside. I grabbed the bed nearest to the window and began unpacking. Shortly afterwards, I was joined by three other girl cadets: Anne Duffin, Janet Ross and Julie Holcombe. Instantly we knew that we would all get on and stick together. We were all in the same boat, not knowing what paths our lives would now take and what challenges lay before us. We went down together to reception to be met by other girl cadets and a number of boy cadets. The smart officer met up with us again. He informed us that we would be going over to the canteen for a cup of tea and then on to the lecture theatre for a course briefing. While he spoke, his face remained serious, but I could detect such a mischievous twinkle in his blue eyes.

"I am PC Lambert; you can call me Mr. Lambert. I am responsible for you now and I will be teaching you everything you need to know. The first thing you need to know is that every member of staff here at Sulhamstead is here to make your life comfortable, you will say hello to everyone you meet from the commandant to the gardener. If I catch anyone being ignored or treated in a rude manner by any of you—you will receive extra drill or punishment that I think fit."

My first lesson towards being a good police officer — no matter who you are dealing with, always treat them with respect and talk to them. This has stayed with me throughout my entire career. I also learnt that I was to be *Girl Cadet 35,* and we were on the *35th Initial Cadet Course.*

The course was to last for four weeks, and we would be based at Sulhamstead apart from an expedition on week three. I was in heaven. Four weeks of running, keep fit, drill (marching) — polishing my shoes — Mr. Lambert even showed us how to get our shoes as shiny as his which I think I almost achieved by the end of four weeks. We went canoeing, swimming, climbing and basically did everything as a team and worked together. This, to me, was absolute heaven. I was living my dream and doing things that I never imagined I would be doing. I thrived on the discipline, the adventure, the companionship of the other cadets and on our beloved leader Tom Lambert.

At the end of the course, our parents were invited to Sulhamstead to watch our passing out parade, and to my utter amazement, I heard my name being called out to receive the *Cadet of the Course Award — Girl Cadet 35 Sedgewick* of the *35th Initial Cadet Course.* I do not think my heart has ever pounded so hard but was also bursting from pride, and I could see my mum and dad sat in the audience with the biggest grins on their faces. I also remember Tom Lambert winking at me and whispering, "Well done, Weed." (This was his nickname for me as a Sedge was a weed and my maiden name is Sedgewick).

MY CADET YEARS

On completion of my course, I was posted for the first year to St Aldates police station in Oxford, where I worked in a variety of departments. For this year, I would be office-bound until I turned eighteen at which point I would be allowed to go out on patrol which seemed forever away.

However, I did spend almost every week either cross-country running for the force team all over the country, swimming training with the other cadets in my area, attending community service at local care homes, and outward bound in mid-Wales which was for me the most exciting holiday for three weeks in the great outdoors, and then I was introduced to the Long Mynd Hike.

Held on the first weekend of October every year (still to this day) it is a 67-mile hike over the Shropshire hills and must be completed in 24-hours.

This was my first real experience of long-distance training, route marching and navigation.

We spent a week training for the event where Tom Lambert led us through the whole course and made us memorize every inch of the way (and I still can remember the entire route to this day). I absolutely loved the event, running most of it and over the years have actually completed it on four occasions, the fastest being in 17-hours and 50 minutes (with a stop in a pub for a whisky and lemonade).

I also was selected for the *Cadet Drill Squad* and attended a three-week course where we performed drill for eight hours a day under the instruction of our leader, Tom. The course was brilliant fun and really did instil so much self-pride into a group of kids from all walks of life. Every second of the day we were immaculately turned out, and our shoes were now as sparkling as Tom's.

The end of the course coincided with the Annual Cadet Parade at Sulhamstead where all of the cadets came together for a parade in front of hundreds of parents and invited guests. The others all marched on and then at the rear of the parade, absolutely in time and looking so slick, our *Drill Squad,* moving as one where we then performed a display containing over thirteen-hundred separate moves and formations.

Even to this day, I feel so lucky to have been chosen to be part of this. Simply the best times.

At the age of eighteen, I transferred over to Cowley police station and started shift work with D Relief going out on patrol mainly around the area where I lived and often watching kids I had been at school with getting arrested. I loved the excitement of night shift although years later hated working them.

I remember being sent over to St Aldates police station one evening in the summer to help out at the annual St Giles Fair. A young sergeant approached me at a briefing and said: "Come on, Carrot Head, let's go for a walk." This young sergeant was Graham Jones, who retired as chief superintendent but became one of my dearest friends along with his wife Madeline, and they both still are to this day and live here on the Isle of Skye. Strange how life weaves its path.

At eighteen and a half, I had to resign from the cadets and apply to join the regular police service as a constable. I really did not want to do anything else except be a cadet. Getting paid to live life to the full with a great bunch of people. I was now looking at earning a living instead of getting paid to live my adventures.

My very first day as a policewoman
after finishing as a cadet only the day before

MARLOW AND HIGH WYCOMBE

Police training these days is totally unrecognizable from my initial course back in 1980. It was all about discipline, drill, fitness, and remembering law — the definitions in parrot-fashion. I found this boring but a necessity to get through my course up at Ryton on Dunsmore.

I was posted to Marlow police station, the only female on a shift of five other men, including my sergeant Adrian Becks. In those days women were definitely a minority in the service, but Sergeant Becks always treated me with the utmost respect. He would often phone my parents and let them know if he felt there was anything wrong, I was not eating properly or something was worrying me. My parents loved him, and he was lovely to them too. I had a four-week period with my tutor constable and then was let loose on my own. I was told in no uncertain terms that I was to walk around town and talk to everyone, get to know every shop keeper, restaurant or bar owner and find out what was happening on my patch. And so that was how I spent the first year of my service doing exactly that. I knew every inch of the town and got to know so many people, many who have remained good friends ever since. During this time, I was also great friends with a young constable from High Wycombe, whom I met at the start of my training course in January 1980. He was a brilliant police officer, worked hard and played harder. He originated from Wales, so was a long way from home and so on every Sunday we were both off he would come over to my mum and dad's house with me for a Sunday roast.

In July 1983, Ian and I were married and are still driving each other mad all these years later. Anne Duffin, one of the other cadets in my room on my very first cadet course was my bridesmaid.

I enjoyed my life as a police officer; however, I hated the night shift and hated confrontation. I loved working with a team and all other aspects of the job but used to get anxious about nightshifts and what each one would bring.

One particular incident in 1982 contributed to this. I was sent out to patrol the areas of Hambleden and Lane End, remote villages deep in the Chilterns on the outskirts of Marlow. In those days working alone was quite normal even for a young female. At about 11.30pm I was tasked to attend an incident on a remote lane just outside the village of Fingest. A report had been received that a car was spotted in a ditch. I immediately attended to discover a vehicle half in a ditch, still warm but with nobody inside. After checking the nearby vicinity, I sat in my patrol car with the blue lights flashing to protect the scene while awaiting the recovery vehicle.

It was while I was sat there that I began to listen to a report coming through on the police radio of a JCB digger being driven erratically on the A40 in Stokenchurch, roughly fifteen miles from my location. As I listened, I can remember thinking, *'Why on Earth would someone be driving a JCB at this time of night?'* Over the course of the next fifteen minutes, more calls were being received from members of the public with reports of damage and destruction along the way. The last location given was at Cadmore End, which was literally just up the road from where I was sitting. My heart sank as I realised that the car in the ditch and JCB were connected.

Sure enough, within a matter of minutes, I was blinded by enormous spotlights on either side of a bright yellow cab. The very same JCB had just arrived and bumped up onto the grass verge in front of the car in the ditch. Inside the cab were two males. I called upon my radio to inform the control room of my own developing situation. I got out of my car and approached the two men who were by now out of the cab and walking towards the car in the ditch with ropes.

I soon discovered that the car belonged to one of the men called Amos, he had been drinking in a nearby pub with his mate, overcooked a bend and lost control of the vehicle sliding into the ditch.

Somehow they got back to his builder's yard on the A40 and decided to attempt recovery with his JCB. There was a strong smell of alcohol on his breath, so I asked him to climb into the rear of my car. Things started to go downhill at this point; he was irritated by my blue lights flashing on the roof of my car, so tried to damage them. Fortunately, I managed to get a call in for assistance on the radio before struggling with him to protect my police car. I asked the other male to help me, but he just thought it was amusing and continued to tie ropes onto the car in the ditch. I repeatedly asked Amos to get into my car, but he was having none of it.

Where was my back up? Basically, nobody really knew the location very well, so it was probably another ten minutes before I saw blue lights rushing towards me to my assistance. Ian had heard my call and responded frantically trying to pinpoint where I was. Amos was arrested and transported over to High Wycombe and eventually charged with a number of road traffic offences including drink driving. I realised how vulnerable I had been, on my own in the middle of the night, in the middle of nowhere dealing with two drunken males. I escaped without any injury but was quite shaken up. Would I be as lucky next time?

In 1986 I decided to try to specialise on a department. I still had my love of animals and had grown up riding horses so did think that I would apply for the mounted section; however, this department was based at Milton Keynes, and I was living in the very lovely riverside town of Marlow and definitely did not wish to relocate.

THE RIVER PATROL UNIT

After a great deal of thought and deliberation, I applied to the Marine Section for a vacancy on the River Patrol Unit.

I loved swimming and loved boating, having owned two boats on the River Thames. Just prior to my application going in I did consider applying for the Underwater Search Unit but did not want to spend my days in cold, nil visibility water looking for dead bodies. I was successful with my application (although I am pretty sure it was only because TVP were desperately trying to get women into what were traditionally seen as male roles).

I was posted to Maidenhead police station, where the River Patrol Unit had its base. My tutor was a long-serving boatman called Bill Harrington, 6'6'' tall; I was a full one-foot one-inch shorter than him. He had a wealth of knowledge on the river and knew everybody. On my first day on the unit, we attended a swimming and life-saving session with the underwater search team who all turned up with their dive kit. I was asked if I would like to have a go and without hesitation agreed.

Even in the swimming pool, I was mesmerized and immediately hooked. I wanted more. I made it very clear over the next few months that I really wanted to become a police diver. Women in the police diving world were unheard of at this time and so this was going to be a big step into the unknown if I was taken on both for me and for TVP.

I spent most days patrolling the non-tidal Thames in either Sitpax or In Valle Tamesis, the two patrol launches. I guess I can equate this to being a village bobby on a very long narrow patch. I really enjoyed meeting the people who lived alongside the river or who were taking holidays there. In those days we had to work shifts on the boats right through the year including a late shift finishing at 2am. I still think of those winter nights where the river would be thundering through under the bridges and over weirs and really having to keep the power on the engine to maintain control, hoping that you did not get something wrapped around the prop at a crucial moment.

One night on leaving the Thames Water moorings at Maidenhead we drove the boat up to Cookham Lock and had to avoid ice flow travelling downstream in the floodwaters. I really did not understand why we worked those shifts as there was absolutely nobody else out on the river and would spend a week working in the freezing cold dark, clocking up hours on the boat's log without seeing a single soul.

MY EARLY DAYS AS A DIVER

Back in 1986, *Health and Safety Legislation* was very different to what it is today and once it became accepted that I was definitely interested in becoming a diver the team got to work on 'preparing' me in readiness for an initial diving course in Sunderland in April 1987.

My first open water dive ever was in the middle of a very fast-flowing River Thames just upstream of Caversham Bridge in Reading. I was buddied to PC John Wood or *Woody* as he was affectionately known; a lovely, gentle guy and a steady and experienced diver. He later became my sergeant on the team but sadly passed away in the late 1990s from a terrible blood disease.

On this day, however, we entered the water from the side of In Valle Tamesis, the larger of the two police boats. We were looking for a possible car. Another river user had spotted a large object on his echo sounder showing up on the river bed.

I can honestly say, I didn't know whether I was upside down or the right way up because of the flow of current. There was nil visibility, but I do remember the green water all around me. I can remember Woody constantly checking up on me and me just responding with a big stupid grin around my mouthpiece and an *'OK'* signal. We never found the object, but I climbed out onto the boat absolutely buzzing. It was the best feeling.

Woody handed me a Codd bottle he had found during the dive as a memento. These were very old bottles with a glass marble stopper held in the pinched neck of the bottle. Along the length of the Thames were areas known for bottles, and often our training dives just happened to take place in or around these areas. I had boxes of old bottles by the time I retired!

My second open water dive was to 30 metres in Datchet Reservoir looking for...another car. This time I was buddied to Alan Penny, who I knew from my Cowley days as a cadet. He always had the biggest smile and lovely blue eyes. I was on the lifeline this time with Alan buddied to me. We were conducting an arc search out into the depths of the reservoir which means that the attendant on the bank held the other end of the lifeline while the diver swam out until the line was tight and swam in an arc backwards and forwards. Each time they got to the end of the arc, the attendant would let out a bit more of the line, and the diver would take up the slack. Obviously the further out you went the more line the diver would be dragging, and I got a bit panicky not really understanding why I was breathing so hard. We were right out at the end of the 75-metre line.

Again though, at the end of the dive, I felt a real surge of adrenalin and excitement at this new type of adventure.

Dive 3—I was on my own on a lifeline under a weir on the River Kennet. I was thrown all over the place and lost both fins which were never found. I still came out with the stupid grin and the biggest buzz of excitement.

My final dive before starting my actual training course was in the River Thames at Clifton Hampden in Oxfordshire on my own on a jackstay (one of the many search patterns we used to search for things underwater). There had been a boat fire, and the investigating officer wanted the river bed around the boat searching in case there were any bodies. The river was flowing hard but with good visibility (well about one metre which was great for the Thames). I managed the whole search until my air started to get low and came out of the water—buzzing and beaming. No bodies to be found, though.

I realized at the end of these four dives that I think the sergeant was actually trying to put me off—I am pleased to say that he failed miserably and I was sent off to Sunderland, one of the two *National Police Dive Schools* to commence an eight-week course.

My course consisted of seven male officers and myself from around the country. The first spoken words to me were from the sergeant, who said, "This isn't a place for women." I have always loved a challenge, and he had thrown down the gauntlet right in the first half-hour. I had eight of the most amazing weeks diving in the docks around Sunderland, the River Tyne in the middle of Newcastle and the North Sea to get our final fifty-metre dive. We were taught search patterns and techniques which would become a routine whenever we entered the water to search for anything.

The course was intensive and exhausting, and I was grateful that I had a high level of strength, fitness and stamina to cope with the demands of carrying the weight of the diving equipment up and down ladders and along river banks. The only time myself or any of the other course members actually received injury was not caused by the diving—behind our accommodation in Sunderland was a big artificial ski slope where from week two we signed up for a ski course. We were all a bit over-enthusiastic, and most of us suffered burns from the many falls and slides while on the skis. Needless to say, our instructors very quickly put a stop to our snowsport activities as you would not be permitted to enter the water with any form of an open wound.

Each week we went deeper and darker. I realized the true meaning of nil visibility in the River Tyne in the old coal quays where the moment your head went under you were surrounded by the blackest water imaginable. It truly was the best fun, I learned so much, mostly about myself and controlling my fears and imagination, and loved the other guys on the course.

At the end of it, I qualified as an HSE (Health & Safety Executive) diver and came top of the course. I also became good friends with the sergeant who had warned me off at the beginning. He really did do me a favour!

My very first body recovery came two days after the end of my course with a suicide victim in Boulters Lock at Maidenhead. It was floating, so I did not have to go through the stress of searching for my first body. I just strapped him onto a stretcher and helped lift him out before taking water samples for the pathologist. These helped to prove whether the person was dead or breathing on entering the water and was obviously more important for murder cases.

Over the next few years, I learnt the ropes of diving with the team. I was expected to dive anywhere there was water, sea, rivers, canals, lakes, reservoirs, ponds and sewage. This was to look for bodies, whether suicide, accidental drowning or murder, weapons used in serious crime or property, the subject of a crime and also included stolen vehicles. Certain dives have always stood out for me including my first dive under a bridge in the Thames at Oxford where the river bed resembled Aladdin's cave; the river bed was gleaming with silver cutlery, coins and jewellery. Any bridge in Oxford was also a major dumping ground for stolen pedal cycles stolen from one of the many colleges. We would often pull out a dozen cycles all perfectly useable again.

During another dive near Didcot, I was sent in to look for a stolen car after tyre tracks were seen on the riverbank leading into the river. It was thick mud on the bottom, no viz and just a miserable dive. After about five minutes I located a car and while waiting for the recovery vehicle to come along I swam along the bank in the mud. I suddenly felt a rectangular box shape and went to lift it but found it too heavy. I called up to the surface to assist me up, and so with the help of them pulling me, I managed to haul this object out of the water where it split open on impact with the bank. It was an old fashioned suitcase, and it was crammed full of coins.

The owners were never found, and so the contents went to Treasure Trove through the coroner. There was £10,000 in old valuable coins. I know that a number of the coins slipped back into the water as I was hauling it out. Maybe one day I'll pay that location a visit again.

Over the years I searched for hundreds of bodies— it was stressful, and it was an aspect of the job that I did not enjoy, not so much the handling of the bodies but the anxiety of the search. I do not think any of the team would say that they enjoyed this part. The worst part was searching in nil viz for an hour, not finding the body, then waiting for your turn again while another diver had a go. By this time, you knew that it was not pleasant down there and you were already cold from the first dive. However, these feelings were immediately forgotten on finding the body, replaced with feelings of relief and elation. I would often find myself talking to the body, almost reassuring it that it was now safe, while waiting for the surface crew to get the stretcher ready for recovery. I truly had no problems when handling or dealing with the dead. I had more of a problem dealing with relatives who often would be standing at the river's edge, waiting for us to find their loved one. I used to find this quite upsetting seeing the grief and waiting, ever hopeful until we delivered their worst nightmare.

Being the smallest on the team, I would often get used for the searches in tight squeezes. On one occasion I was lowered down into a half-flooded storm drain to recover the rotting body of a lady who had been murdered by her husband on a private estate in Denham in Buckinghamshire. As I was trying to bag her up in this very restricted concrete underground box, I felt something nudge the side of my mask and discovered it was the skin from five perfectly formed toes floating around.

After every dive, all of our equipment would be decontaminated back at our base, and on this last occasion, my drysuit was covered in small bits of very rotten skin. After pressure hosing my suit, we realized that this flesh was now splattered over our cars parked in the carpark. Not nice and a lesson learned.

Many of our recoveries were of children who were always obviously more difficult, not only because we were looking for a little person, but the search was always accompanied by whole families and the press hoping to get a picture.

Fortunately, we had devised methods of recovery from water that meant that by the time the body was out of the water, it was already on a stretcher under cover. In the summer you could more or less guarantee that on a Sunday afternoon we would get called out, always to look for teenage boys. Boys just wanting to cool off by swimming across a gravel pit and underestimating their fitness or the distance.

Our other role was to search for explosives in confined spaces, so by that, I mean sewers and tunnels. Normally, before a visit by a VIP or someone known to have a terrorist threat against them, we were responsible for everything below ground. The busiest week every year was for Royal Ascot week where we had nine miles of culverts, sewers and tunnels to search ahead of the royal carriage procession. It is interesting that even now when I visit some of the places we used to search, I can still remember what we were searching for and why. The same applies to the rivers; I can go to a location and remember exactly what we were looking for.

I used to hate diving in the Grand Union Canal at Slough; it was always muddy, black and full of junk that had been thrown in over the years. On one particular dive, we were asked to search for a knife used in a fatal stabbing. While the diver was searching the canal bed, the rest of the team were on the bank attending to the diver and coordinating the search. Throughout the search, we were pestered constantly by a local nutter who kept asking what we were looking for. He was politely told to bugger off on a number of occasions. However, he kept coming back and was really becoming annoying. He again asked what we were looking for where he was told under no uncertain terms that it was none of his business and would he, please go away. He then said, "Are you looking for this?" and thrust his hand towards us brandishing a knife. When asked where he got it from he informed us that he had found it lying approximately 20-feet behind us. Lesson learned— always search the area on the bank before putting the diver in.

While diving in the Thames and Kennet in Reading on a training dive, I was attending the diver when we heard a loud splash only to see that a local drunk had thrown himself in from a nearby bridge and was struggling to stay afloat. We quickly called the diver to the surface who swam over to the drunk and dragged him out. We dried him off and sat him in the lorry to warm up with a cup of soup while we continued with the dive. When we returned to the lorry, the drunk had vanished with all our loose change. Another lesson—don't rescue drunks and certainly don't leave them unsupervised!

In 1992 I became the first female dive supervisor in the country and so was now able to coordinate and plan any diving operations which I thoroughly enjoyed doing; although at times found it very stressful when deploying divers in fast-flowing water or where there were snag hazards like trees and cars. It was always a relief to get the divers out safely and with bodies or property recovered. I really did take my supervisory role very seriously as I did not want anything to go wrong during the dive. If things go wrong underwater, it normally resulted in serious injury or death.

I truly was enjoying every aspect of my career on the diving team. I loved working with an amazing team and felt it was the best job in the force. But another part of me felt that I was halfway through a police career, could I qualify as a sergeant and maybe one day run the team. I sat my sergeants' exam in 1993 and passed it. This, to me, was a miracle because I found studying law was so boring. *Diving Rules and Regulations* were far more exciting. The good news was that I was promoted in January 1994, the bad news was I had to leave the team and do a two-year stint back out on the streets before I could specialize. I spent these two years at High Wycombe, where I was responsible for about fifteen young officers all looking to me for guidance and leadership. The last time I had performed any proper police work was in 1986 when everything was under the auspices of *Judges Rules;* now it was PACE *(Police and Criminal Evidence Act)*, a completely different legal system; talk about the blind leading the blind. I hated shift work again; I hated nights and really did not enjoy the work. My heart was submerged beneath the surface of the Thames, which seemed so far away.

During the summer of 1995, I learned that Woody—who was the sergeant on the team—was also going to apply for promotion and was looking to leave the team to gain street experience in readiness for promotion. Soon after, the post of *Sergeant: Underwater Search* was advertised in the Weekly Orders.

I applied straight away and attended the interview in November 1995. The interview ran really smoothly; I had done everything in my power to prepare for it. It was also a great feeling to know more about the questions being asked than the people on the panel who were asking them. I learned the very same day that I had been successful and so all that I had to do was wait until January when my two years as a sergeant on the streets was completed.

*Me searching under the ice in the Grand Union Canal
looking for evidence connected to a murder*

SERGEANT IN CHARGE –
UNDERWATER SEARCH

January 1996 and I was now the sergeant in charge of the *Underwater Search Unit* at Sulhamstead. The first female in the country to hold such a post.

I thought I had the best job in the police before as a constable, but now I knew that this was the best. Not only was I able to continue diving and doing all the dirty, cold stuff that I loved from being a constable on the team, but I now had a say in decision-making and the running of the team—the best of both worlds. I had a great team of divers, all whom I already knew from my previous time on the team. They were all enthusiastic, professional and proud to be there.

I was fortunate in that I already knew and understood exactly what the job entailed so the handover was straightforward, and I just had to get to grips with budgets and senior management. Fortunately, I had tremendous support from the civilian support staff at my departmental headquarters who literally were the backbone of all the specialist departments, and I know that without their expertise, everything would have ground to a halt. I used to love visiting the offices in Bicester for a cuppa and a catch up on the gossip with Mary and Carole.

I always insisted on the best clothing and equipment for the team. Our lives depended on it. We were outdoors in all weathers, and often the coldest place was above the surface and not where you would expect, down below. It was a struggle, to begin with, to get the clothing store's manager on my side. He and a team visited a dive site at my request on a very cold winter's day standing there for hours in freezing wet conditions; they soon realized that I was actually very reasonable with my requests. Chris, the store manager, was a lovely guy and I always paid him a visit when I was up at Bicester. It paid off because very shortly afterwards we had the very best Gortex wet weather gear and thermals money could buy.

When I became the sergeant on the team it was at a time when the police service was looking at making cutbacks. Especially under scrutiny were small, expensive departments and the *Underwater Search Team* was a very expensive small department. I realized that we would need to utilize our skills in other areas to make ourselves invaluable.

As if by coincidence, a call came into my office from an officer at Newbury. They had a situation in an upstairs flat where a decomposing body had been found. The body was in such a state that the undertakers refused to enter the flat to remove the body. Would we do it?

I immediately agreed, and we arrived at the scene in our dive lorry. Three of us got kitted up in drysuits, breathing apparatus and gloves and entered the flat to be faced with the decomposing remains of a male whose body had gone into meltdown. Fortunately, we were all sealed off from the stench, maggots, flies and body fluids everywhere, and just got on with the job, bagging him up before carrying him out to the awaiting undertakers' vehicle. As a result of this first request, it then snowballed, and every week we were called out to decomposing bodies in buildings.

One, in particular, stands out for me. We were called to a block of flats in Langley. A body had been found in one of the top-floor flats and was in meltdown mode. We rode the lift and then approached the flat. Fortunately, we were fully kitted up, the body was in a bad state, and the flies were feasting. This was a male, a very tall male. We managed to bag him up and then carried the bag out onto the communal landing. And then it hit us. How were we going to get him down eleven or twelve storeys? It would be hot, exhausting work to take him down the stairs. Let's get him in the lift. We called the lift, the doors opened, and we were then faced with the next problem. The floor space in the lift was tiny. There was no way we could lie him down. We agreed between the three of us to stand him up with each of us propping him up in the body bag. So, there we were, three police officers in full drysuits, gloves and breathing apparatus hugging a dead body in a bright yellow body bag emblazoned with large black letters, the words *'Bio Hazard'* on the side, riding down in the tiny lift. All was going well until at floor six; the lift bell pinged, the lift lurched to a halt, the doors opened and in swaggered a young black man with masses of dreadlocks and attitude. He stopped dead in his tracks just as the doors closed behind him. We all nodded hello to him and for the next six floors had a job keeping it together as he gagged and retched with the stench. It must have been horrendous for him, but it was quite funny for us.

We developed systems of recovery, ensuring that each poor soul we recovered was recovered in a dignified and respectful manner while also managing to keep as much of the body intact for evidential purposes. Very soon after, police forces throughout the country were getting in touch to learn from our recovery techniques. TVP invested in this.

Also, we were supplied with a purpose-built vehicle and lightweight breathing apparatus instead of the steel diving cylinders we had used on the first few recoveries.

I was involved in so many decomposing body recoveries; they really were much worse than underwater recoveries purely because of the state of decomposition that they were in, stuff that nightmares are made of.

Out of all the bodies that I helped to recover, there were only two that caused me to gag and want to really hurry up with the recovery. One was a morbidly obese gentleman who had literally melted into his floor. His body fluids and the maggots were dropping through into the flat below onto a dining room table. The family were eating at the time it was first noticed.

The other was a tiny lady whose head had fallen off in the bathroom sink. As I recover the head from the sink, her jaw bone fell off into this gloopy mess lying beneath in the sink, disappearing below the surface. Trust me; I really did not want to put my hand in to search for it. The only thing to hand was a plastic soap dish. Thankfully I managed to retrieve the jaw bone on the first dip in with the soap dish. On the way home from both, I had to stop the vehicle, get out and breathe fresh air. I could not eat anything for the rest of the day in both cases.

I always found it very upsetting to know that the poor souls we recovered from houses were very much alone. If they had family and friends who cared, the bodies would not have been left unfound for weeks and sometimes months.

The next skill we then learned was rope access. This was definitely out of my comfort zone, but being a diver, I had a good faith in my equipment, and this got me through each climb. We used these skills to safely recover suicide victims who had ended their lives by hanging. We could now safely climb up to them, attach our own ropes and lower them gently and intact to the awaiting undertakers. We also developed the climbing systems to help with security searching on rooftops and sides of buildings and bridges.

Our main daily work was searching, slow,

fingertip searching, and we were good at it from the years of underwater searching.

We began to be used for fingertip searching at serious crime scenes, indoors as well as outside. Then we got a call to assist with a raid on a drug dealer's house, following the heavies who forced the door in, we then went in to search the premises. We tore it apart and found a big stash of drugs and weapons. This became another string to our bow. We even became qualified to smash down the doors on arrival.

Our days were full of searching and recovering both above and below the water. The team quite rightly got a reputation as the team to go to if you needed something found and so we were called out on many high-profile cases. By now our workload was showing that we were spending half our time above water; conducting specialized searches, so it only seemed appropriate to change the name from the *Underwater Search Team* to the *Specialist Search and Recovery Team* or SSRT.

*On my Rope Access Course, just about to swing out
from the top of the control tower*

My team at the end of my service demonstrating our skills. From left to right: Craig Newton, wearing CBRN (Chemical, Biological, Radioactive and Nuclear) search equipment; Rupert Jones, wearing confined space search equipment; Mark Roddam, wearing body recovery suit; Andy Clark, wearing diving equipment; Me, in police uniform; Nick Peck, in surface demand diving equipment; Billy Cairney, as a boat handler and attendant; Pete Darling, ready to smash down doors; Martin Armstrong, in rope access equipment

HERBAL SEP

During these early months on the team as the sergeant, my husband Ian who was now a *Tactical Dog Handler* received an injury as a result of a nasty assault and had to leave the police service as a result of these injuries. Our lives were turned upside down. Ian actually went through two years of *Post Traumatic Stress* and depression following on from this until retraining as an artist, finishing with a first in ceramics and fine arts three years later. He did so well, not being either an academic or an artist. I was just very grateful that during those very dark two years, I was doing a job I adored. It could have been very different otherwise.

Ian suffered an injury to the neck, causing a narrowing of his spinal column. This causes daily nerve pain through both arms and at times has been quite debilitating for him.

Shortly after Ian retired from the police, we received a call from Cas and Sonja, two dear friends who live in Switzerland. Sonja had slipped a disc in her back and had visited a herbalist living high up in the Swiss Alps called Herbal Sep. She had visited only on one occasion where Sep correctly identified the problem with Sonja's back and suggested a treatment for it that appeared to be working well. Cas and Sonja asked if Ian would like to fly over to Switzerland to see Herbal Sep. I could not get leave, so Ian was to go on his own.

Twenty-four hours before the flight, I managed to get some time off, flying out with Ian and totally surprising Cas and Sonja who were not expecting me. We were whisked straight off up into the Alps, to a modern apartment block where Herbal Sep lived in a top-floor apartment.

A wizened older man opened the door before leading us through to a large room overlooking the mountains. A hard-backed chair in the middle of the floor was the only item of furniture. Sep could only speak in an ancient Swiss dialect, so Cas and Sonja translated for us. Ian sat down on the chair and soon Herbal Sep was weaving his hands around Ian without actually touching his body, all the while making little growls. I found this fascinating, even more so when Cas explained at the end that Sep's diagnosis was completely accurate. He suggested a treatment and went on to tell Ian that he would always have an eagle flying over him for protection.

I was pretty impressed, to say the least. Cas had never met Sep before, and Sonja had only met him once and had not discussed Ian with him, she had only made an appointment for him. I was suffering from a right knee injury at the time which neither Cas or Sonja was aware of and just wondered whether Sep would be able to identify it. Cas asked if he would have a look at me, and he agreed. For the next fifteen minutes, Herbal Sep weaved his hands just above the surface of my skin. He snarled and growled, leaping away and snarling even more. I actually began to get worried, had he found something terribly wrong with me? This continued until I could stand it no longer. "Cas, please will you ask him what is wrong with me?" Cas spoke to Sep, and as he did, I saw the colour drain out of his face. Cas turned back to me and said, "Sep says that you are surrounded by the souls of hundreds of bodies. He just doesn't understand why."

I replied, "Please just tell him what I do for a living, and can he remove them?"

Cas then explained what my job was on a daily basis with Sep listening, nodding his head and the occasional *"Ahh."*

For the next fifteen minutes, Sep got to work on my invisible friends, snarling and growling, pulling these poor souls away from me. At the end of this, he explained that they were with me because I had helped them. They were not harming me but were draining my energy. He instructed me to pull an imaginary bubble over myself whenever I dealt with a dead body in the future. I was absolutely speechless, and the hairs were standing up on the back of my neck. This guy had no way of knowing.

He then diagnosed my bad right knee and suggested I regularly soak in a bath of milk and honey (Boots do a good milk and honey bubble bath, so it had to do!). I then asked him if I had a guardian bird.

Sep said something and Cas replied, "Yes, a

pigeon."

"A pigeon? I don't want a feckin' pigeon!"

Cas apologised and said, 'A white pigeon, a bird of peace, a dove."

I was happy with a dove! This whole incident had a lasting effect on me, and from that moment on, I always pulled my imaginary bubble over myself when dealing with bodies safe under the protective eye of my white pigeon. Herbal Sep also gave me a ceramic dove which still sits on the windowsill in my bedroom keeping an eye on me.

MAJOR DISASTER
BODY RECOVERY

In 1999 I approached the *Emergency Planning Officer* at headquarters and asked what would happen if a jumbo jet crashed in the Thames Valley area. Who would be responsible for picking up the pieces? Bearing in mind that we had Heathrow at the edge of our patch with the ditching area in a reservoir actually inside our force area. I was informed that my team would do the job. I was a bit taken aback, to say the least as there were only eight of us on the team plus a civilian dive technician. Then out of the blue, I received a call from Hertfordshire police who were running a *Major Disaster Body Recovery Course.* Would I like to go along as an observer? I leapt at the chance and the following week I found myself recovering fake body parts from an air crash at Luton airport as part of the course.

Following on from my course, over the next four years, I trained ninety officers to become proficient in recovering body parts from all types of disaster, man-made or natural.

A day after the first course, I received a call. There had been a very nasty traffic accident in Wokingham involving two vehicles, both of which had burst into flames killing all four passengers. Could we attend? In this instance, an elderly couple were driving over to their daughter's house who just happened to be a police officer on her way out for early turn. The parents were going to babysit. Along come two lads racing towards them after a long night out clubbing and wiped them out. End of story.

We spent a whole day recovering charred remains from both vehicles—four people—thirty-two body parts. Rightly or wrongly, it was hard not to let your emotions run riot while recovering the remains of the two male offenders who had wiped out the lives of two innocent people. The nearby Sainsbury's offered us a breakfast halfway through the morning—crispy bacon sandwiches! It really did not go down too well at the time.

Within a day of finishing the second course, I received a call to say that a light aircraft had crashed high up on the Downs at Lambourne, killing all four people on board. Could I attend and organize what needed to be done? On arrival, I realized that the first problem was communications. Due to the location, we could not use radios or mobile phones and had to keep running back to a nearby farm to use a landline if we needed anything. The second problem was the weather, icy gales and snow and the third problem was the location, in a woodland in the middle of a muddy field high up on the downs. The press were there all edging to get the shot; it was like working in a goldfish bowl in clear view of everyone. Eventually, we managed to get the press moved away so that they couldn't get the desired snap of one of us recovering a body part.

The four people on board were the pilot, a ten-year-old girl (the flight was her 10th birthday present), her dad and her uncle. Somewhere along the way, the plane developed a problem and plummeted to the earth. Four people, ninety-seven body parts, hanging from trees, in the undergrowth, everywhere. The little girl was the only one intact, and I will never forget her little hand sticking up through the wreckage. It took us five days to complete the search and recovery, and we received high praise at the end from both the pathologist and the coroner for our system of recovery and recording of each part, making their jobs so much easier.

Air Accident Investigation discovered that the plane had lost altitude very suddenly, immediately the pilot tried to regain height by pulling the lever back but overcooked it. This sudden thrust upwards, over-strained parts of the plane which began to fall apart under the stress. If he had responded more gently, the plane might well have survived intact. This subsequently became part of training for new pilots.

After the third course, everyone held their breath — it seemed that we were jinxed. Every time we ran a course, a disaster would follow. In a way, this was good experience in that it gave us a chance as a team to practice our skills for real and also demonstrating just how time-consuming it was even for a small incident, especially completion of the paperwork.

The third course came and went without incident, and we all breathed again. The fourth course was held and nothing until 6th November, 2004 when I received a call to attend the level crossing at Ufton Nervet in Berkshire during the early evening. The 1735 Intercity train from Paddington to Plymouth had collided with a stationary vehicle positioned on the level crossing killing the driver of the car, the train driver and five passengers. Approximately one-hundred people were injured, eleven seriously who had to be cut free from the wreckage. All eight coaches were derailed. It was chaos when I arrived with emergency vehicles everywhere. I knew that I would be calling out my team again and got to work getting them to Sulhamstead, which was literally three miles away. I met them all at Sulhamstead at 0400 and briefed them, two teams, to recover six bodies (one of the bodies, a 9-year-old girl had been carried out of the wreckage by her father immediately after the incident).

We had to work in unison with the *Fire and Rescue*, and railway officials while the carriages were airlifted up so that we could access beneath them to recover the remains of the victims. It was difficult and dangerous work and throughout there was an urgency to get the line reopened as soon as possible. It took us four days to recover the bodies, the body parts and personal property. The driver of the car on the level crossing had parked there deliberately wanting to end his own life. Through his own actions, he did not think that the consequences would end the lives of six others. The recovery of the train driver had an impact on all of us. Following the impact with the vehicle, the train was de-railed, leaving the tracks and eventually coming to a halt, embedded in a high gravel embankment. The driver was literally crushed to death under the weight of the gravel. His arms were in the air with a look of horror on his face. We had to dig the rest of his body free. Most of us shed a tear while working with his recovery. I can remember as we carried his body out on the stretcher seeing the Fire and Rescue guys remove their helmets out of respect. We did not shed a tear while recovering the car driver though still afforded him the same dignity of recovery. Somewhere out there was a father, mother or relative who loved him and would miss him. Very sad. I worked through twenty-eight hours on the first day at the scene and spent a week trying to come down from my overactive mind running away with so many thoughts. It was exhausting work but at the same time very satisfying knowing that we were helping the relatives get their loved ones back.

The Lambourne air crash recovering one of the bodies

THE TSUNAMI

By 2004 Ian had been living on the Isle of Skye for three years with my mum and dad and had opened a very successful art gallery there, while also running bed and breakfast from the house.

I long-distance commuted the 640 miles each way journey every four weeks from Marlow on my long weekends. I was spending Christmas there, right through until the New Year. I woke on Boxing Day and watched in horror at the developing news—a massive tsunami had wiped out the lives of dozens of people in the Indian Ocean. Very rapidly dozens became hundreds, then thousands and then hundreds of thousands. It was being predicted as the worst natural disaster in history.

Triggered by an undersea megathrust earthquake registering a magnitude of 9.3 on the Richter scale, a series of 30 metre high tsunamis hit the coastlines of Banda Aceh in Indonesia, Sri Lanka, India and Thailand, plus other countries further afield. It also caused the entire Earth to vibrate one centimetre.

The tsunami hit the south-west coast of Thailand with the wave reaching on average six metres. It also struck during a high tide increasing its devastating effect. Just under 5400 people were killed in Thailand although the actual estimate was nearer to 8100—reported missing people never recovered.

The province at Phang Nga was the most heavily

affected including the beautiful Khao Lak beach area with its many luxurious beach hotels crammed full of foreign holidaymakers. This area also has many small fishing villages where hundreds of locals lost their lives. At Khao Lak, the first wave created an initial depression called a tsunami drawback or disappearing sea effect, which then creates an even larger second wave. News began to filter through that there were also many Britons who may have been killed (140 in total).

While watching the developing news I immediately knew that I would somehow be involved. A massive disaster abroad involving British nationals. This was what I had been training for since 1999. Sure enough within 24-hours, I received a call from the emergency planning office at HQ. Would I be able to get a team of fifteen together to go out to Thailand to assist with the victim identification? There was no question about it. I put out an email immediately to the team and immediately was inundated with positive responses from trained officers desperate to get involved.

I arrived back in TVP with a list of thirty officers who would be available to travel at short notice to Thailand at any time within the next three months. This was then whittled down to the fifteen as required. From that point on, I was literally running flat out, getting everything ready. I was given a blank cheque from the then Chief Constable Peter Neyroud, who was absolutely brilliant. He supported me above and beyond what I expected and trusted me to get the job done. I knew we would be working in hot, humid conditions, so I wanted the best clothing for this. Cotswold Outdoors at Reading had the highest sales nationally as a result of my visit. They kitted us out with t-shirts, shorts, trousers, hats, sun cream, boots, shoes, pants, sunglasses; you name it. Then I had to get the forensic kit together, Tyvek white suits, gloves, disinfectant wipes, overshoes. Simply tons of kit but all absolutely necessary for the work we would be doing. During this time, we each attended psychological assessments, doctors examinations, briefings and more briefings. We had vaccinations for every disease known to man. We were given briefings from officers who had already been out there and had come back, filling our minds full of the horrors we would be facing and the conditions we would be working in.

Buildings in Khao Lak hit by the wave

Tsunami devastation Khao Lak,
this was once a luxurious beach resort

Khao Lak

All that was left of a beautiful beachside hotel

Entire holiday resorts were wiped out

SITE 1 AND 2

Our team flew out to Bangkok in late February from Heathrow. We were travelling in business class with Qantas, and I found myself sat next to a lovely diamond dealer from Australia. I tried chatting him up in the hope that he might slip me a spare gem or two, but the only nuggets I got out of him were nuggets of information all about the diamond mining industry in Australia.

The heat in Bangkok was stifling on arrival. I don't think I had ever experienced such intense humidity in my life before. We then had to catch a short internal flight to Phuket airport arriving at about midnight. We were based in a hotel on the west coast of Phuket Island that had escaped with only minor damage. We were all too wide awake by now to sleep, so had a few beers in the bar and held an impromptu briefing. We were due to be up at five to be on site up in Mai Khao for 7am. I can remember crawling into bed at about 2am thinking that it was all a dream.

Following the tsunami in Thailand, the Thai authorities realized that they would be dealing with thousands of dead bodies, including many foreign nationals all celebrating Christmas holidays at the many beach resorts. The Thai government put out a request for international help and as a result police officers and forensic experts including dentists and pathologists from the UK, USA, Canada, Finland,

Norway, Sweden, Denmark, France, Germany, Italy, Holland, Thailand, China, Japan, Australia and New Zealand responded.

In the meantime, two temporary mortuary sites were set up: Site 1 at Wat Yan Yao, Takua Pa, a fishing town at the north end of Khao Lak Beach. This was a Buddhist temple that was handed over by the monks to become a temporary mortuary and Site 2 at Mai Kao at the north end of Phuket Island. This was a purpose-built temporary mortuary flown in by the Norwegians as a response to the disaster. The Thai government also instructed that any body found should be wrapped in polythene bags and taken to one of the two sites. At Site 1, there were probably over 2500 bodies at the beginning all just lying in the sun in their polythene bags cooking nicely.

As you can imagine the flies were straight in there, the bodies were in meltdown, and the stench was horrendous. Something had to be done.

First, dry ice was used to cool down the bodies to no effect, then formaldehyde to try and preserve the bodies. This was also totally ineffective, they were still basting well, so large refrigerated containers were brought in, and the bodies were placed in these and frozen until each body was to be removed to go through the identification procedures. Each body was given a unique reference number, a photograph was taken and on the outside of each container was a plan showing where each numbered body was within that container. This would have been a good system, but only if the officers using the system fully understood how it worked.

At Site 1 there were sixty-four containers, each containing eighty bodies. At Site 2 there were seventy-two.

Just prior to our deployment a number of containers at Site 1 that had initially been placed alongside the canal in Takua Pa all malfunctioned causing the temperature within to build up and the bodies again to suffer meltdown. As a result, the body fluids were leaking out into the canal system, which is where the locals were using for daily washing. Obviously this was becoming hazardous and unpleasant for the locals so new containers were brought in, and the bodies in the defective containers had to be relocated.

We had been briefed that we would be working at Site 1 throughout our deployment. This was to be our workplace for the next month; however it didn't quite work out that way. Just prior to our arrival the authorities discovered that the soil of Site 1 was heavily impregnated with asbestos and so we were diverted back down to Site 2.

5am saw fifteen bleary-eyed TVP officers stagger down for breakfast before heading off in the minibus for whatever was to be thrown at us. Site 2 was a complete contrast to Site 1. The entrance was off a busy dual carriageway and a mile before you reached it you passed a sign warning of *'Bodies'*. I can promise you; there was no need for that sign;

you could smell nothing else.

You then passed through a long driveway in between the *Wall of Remembrance* created to stop relatives hanging about at the main gates. I used to hate this wall because while dealing with the dead they were firmly dead, by looking at the photos on the wall, the bodies became living people again, and it became all too moving and real, plus day after day hundreds of distraught relatives would be there crying and pleading to have their loved ones found.

Site 2 was a modern temporary mortuary site made up of three very large portacabins and seventy-two containers. It was much larger than Site 1 and much hotter.

Our rest area was a line of green tents reminiscent of Mash and where we proudly raised the TVP flag. There were proper toilets and a canteen where the food was excellent. Those first few days were spent defrosting containers in preparation for the identification process and moving bodies through the system back to the containers.

At both sites, the system was the same: fingerprints, post mortem, DNA and odontology. The forensic experts from around the world were truly amazing, and I take my hat off to them.

It was bad enough for us just to be climbing into the containers and dragging the bodies out; the forensic teams were nose to decomposing flesh every day.

While at Site 2, we decided to visit the local temple

where the Buddhist monks lived and in whose grounds Site 2 was situated. The head monk had blessed the mortuary site after it first opened. We each wanted to be blessed by this monk. It was amazing. This monk who lived in utter poverty was sat in this ramshackle hut, he was dressed in bright orange robes with a shaven head and was sat cross-legged on the floor awaiting our arrival. We knelt before him while he said prayers and splashed each of us with water.

While waiting for my turn my eyes adjusted to the dim light and realised he had the biggest ghetto blaster sitting on a shelf above where he sat, and he was actually surrounded by every electrical gadget known to man. His prayers were interrupted by the ringing of his mobile phone going off. It was quite unreal and a little bit like a comedy sketch.

At the end of the week, we were to report back to Site 1. We understood that conditions were below basic. It was also an hour and a half travelling time from our hotel. On the very first drive down, we passed through many pockets of devastation, but nothing prepared us for the view across Khao Lak as we hit the viewpoint before dropping down onto the coast road. What should have been the most amazing palm tree-lined beach scene was a war zone. It looked like it had been flattened, then picked up and dropped and flattened again. Mile after mile of destruction, ghostly hotels, windows smashed in, walls knocked down, swimming pools filled with dark brown filthy water, and debris everywhere. I will never forget that moment in time as fifteen apprehensive British police officers, a long way from home, stood in silence, unable to speak, unable to take it all in and very much aware that we were looking at the site of something far bigger than anything we could ever have imagined. The scale of devastation was beyond belief.

As we drove through the tourist town of Khao Lak, the main road was still covered in sand washed in over a mile from the beach from eight weeks before and to our right a solitary police launch sat in the middle of a field washed in with the same sand. Watermarks up to the second storey of hotel rooms were all that remained to show just how high the tsunami wave actually reached. Further north refugee camps had been set up for the locals which are still inhabited to this day. Everywhere were piles of twisted debris as the locals attempted to tidy up and get their lives back into some sort of order. Sadly, everywhere you looked were personal belongings, clothes, flip-flops, driving licenses, and fluffy toys.

We arrived at Site 1 driving under an elaborate entranceway covered in gold leaf. Getting out of the van at 6.30 in the morning, the intensity of the heat hit us. The ever-present smell of death was lingering in the air though we were getting used to that now, and we walked over to our rest area outside the main temple area. We were told it was going to be basic. That was an understatement, squat toilets, no washing facilities and nowhere to eat.

Decontamination was in a tin washing-up bowl where we used to swish our boots on leaving the site before dropping our Tyvek suits. We would work with the bodies for a few hours, step out and decontaminate before sitting under our Coca Cola tent canopy to escape death. Unfortunately, this was placed right beneath the crematorium chimney which was fired up most days covering us with the ashes of the very same dead.

As in Site 2, our daily work would consist of selecting a container at the end of each day, defrosting it to 3 degrees so that the bodies became workable. The admin team would then produce the paperwork for each body in that container. The next morning we would collect the paperwork, find the body and wheel it over to the entrance of the mortuary awaiting the ID process. As I mentioned before if the bodies were in the places indicated on the door plan, it was a straightforward walk in, find the body bag and haul it out. However, most days were spent up on shelves in amongst twenty to thirty defrosting decomposing bodies searching for the one with the body number that matched the paperwork that had not been put in its correct place; and if it was a small child or baby, it made the task even harder searching for it in amongst very large north European males.

From there, the experts would take fingerprints, conduct a post mortem, take DNA and dental impressions. We would then put the body back to bed in its respective container and freeze it back down. All of the forensic information obtained would be entered into a computer which would be linked to police computers in countries all over the world.

All over the world worried relatives were reporting their loved ones missing. The local police would take full descriptions including any artificial implants such as pacemakers, knees, hips (they all had unique serial numbers), unique scars and marks, get dental records, any fingerprint history and DNA. This would all be fed into the same computer back home. The computer would do its stuff and *bingo!* If there was a match, we had a positive ID.

The information and medical evidence would then be presented to a panel of high-ranking police officers *(the Identification Commission)* from around the world. If they agreed that there was sufficient evidence (there had to be three points of match to satisfy them) then the body with its proper name and identification would be released to family members if it was a Thai or to the respective embassy of the country from where the victim came from.

Our life on-site was hot, uncomfortable and non-stop. It was interesting to see that some of the officers on my team who had never handled dead bodies before, were at first reluctant and held back, letting those of us used to handling death on a daily basis do the work. By about day three, the heat was so intense. Where were these officers to be found? In the chilled containers with the dead bodies keeping cool. Death was no longer an issue. Our team were soon involved in every stage of the identification process.

The post mortem process was very different to post mortems as we know them here in the UK. The bodies were stripped of any clothing left on, most clothing had been ripped off by the force of the waves anyway, and so nearly all the bodies were naked. The bodies were then cleaned with water from a bucket and old credit cards to scrape the mud off. The bodies were examined for tattoos, scars and deformities and obviously any artificial parts. The sex, height and weight were also taken. They were also examined for suspicious injuries. Every body was battered and bruised from being carried along with the wave before impacting with vehicles and buildings. They wanted to make sure there were no obvious stab wounds or gunshot wounds, the body being secreted amongst the tsunami dead. One of our lads helped out with the post mortems frequently helping in all stages of the post mortem. This was hard stomach-turning work and Chris Bennington, I take my hat off to you.

Fingerprinting was horrific to watch but fascinating. Watching the Thai forensic experts was a lesson in techniques not seen in this country but now widely used. They would, first of all, try to lift fingerprints directly from the finger with traditional methods using either ink or powder, rolling out the impression on fingerprint forms. These bodies had been submerged in water, subjected to extreme heat and were decomposing; therefore, the skin was wrinkled and shrunk. If a print could not be obtained by the traditional method, they would then inject saline solution under the skin of each finger to plump it up giving it a more normal shape enabling a print to be lifted. If these methods failed then the finger would be submerged in boiling water for about fifteen seconds, the skin would slough off; the expert would then place the skin on their own finger enabling a print to be rolled out. The skin would then be returned to its body. As I said, horrific to watch but very successful and a system now used in this country.

DNA involved cutting a 7cm length of the femur bone from each victim. These bones were then sent to China for DNA testing. Shortly after our arrival the Chinese stopped testing and informed us that 1000 samples had been lost, so one of our first tasks at Site 1 was to reprocess 1000 bodies through the DNA system where the samples were then sent to the War Crimes Commission for analysis.

Odontology was nothing like the treatment in your own dental surgeries, thank goodness and again quite horrific to watch but absolutely necessary. The team of dentists at Site 1 were crazy New Zealanders. Despite the nature of their work, the room was always full of laughter and jokes, though never at the expense of the victims.

The main mortuary, where everything else took place, was affectionately called the 'Opera House' because every day it was filled with the sound of music and singing—mainly led by the Dutch. At first it all seemed a bit surreal, but soon you realized that this was the way that they dealt with the horrors facing them each day. The site itself was hazardous; there was no decontamination, no lighting, bones sticking through body bags waiting to impale the unsuspecting officer about to move it, dogs running everywhere and chickens. One dog was adopted by the team which we called Digit for reasons I won't go into.

When we first arrived at Site 1, Kev, our Detective Inspector who came out as part of the team, asked if a risk assessment had been completed for the site. The response from the Australian site commander at the time was, "Yep and it's fucking risky!" Say no more.

Our daily lives were now breakfast at 5am, onto the site by 7am, sweltering heat and running about until about 5.30pm then drive home arriving at about 7pm. The drive back always seemed to take forever, and you would be trying to get some sleep while thinking that the guys on either side of you smelled really bad. At some stage later into the journey, you realized that it was yourself that smelt so bad. I could barely live with the stench of death on my skin. I would literally get back to my hotel room, strip off at the door, place everything in the laundry bag and call for laundry...and then cringe at the thought of the poor laundry staff opening the bag to wash my kit.

Despite being surrounded by hundreds of dead bodies on a daily basis, it never bothered me. I really was not affected by it though the enormity of it still took my breath away. The dead bodies were just that: dead. Just occasionally, during a quiet moment, it would hit me: me and hundreds of corpses all around. I certainly pulled a double reinforced bubble over me on site.

At Site 1 a large photo board had been erected prior to our arrival with photos of all the dead bodies. The board was right outside the admin office and alongside our rest area. The photo board was a waste of time because no matter whether you were white, black, yellow, the tsunami had transformed everyone into a bloated green rotting body; unless there was a unique deformity or scar on the face that was clearly obvious. Nonetheless, everyday the photo board was surrounded by crowds of relatives and friends searching for their missing loved ones and often it was heartbreaking to watch. It was the living emotions that I just could not come to terms with.

One day we finished slightly early and decided to drive down to a local beach to wash off before our long drive home. We all dived into the water and just swam about for about half an hour, and then I decided to walk along the beach to dry off before getting into the van. As I was walking in the sand lost in my own thoughts, my attention was drawn to a small fluffy object lying in the sand. On closer inspection, I discovered that it was a one-eared fluffy bunny. Before I knew it, this little fluffy bunny had reduced me to floods of tears. I guess knowing that this was probably the favourite toy of one of the many victims. It just brought it home to me at that moment. I often wished that I had picked him up and brought him home but thought he belonged there. I felt very sad to leave him lying in the sand watching me walk away and sadly, I do think of that bunny often. It was a very poignant moment for me.

*The sign on the main road into Site 2
at Mai Khao on Phuket*

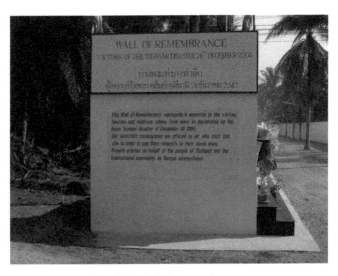

The Wall of Remembrance

*The Coca Cola tent was our rest area
right underneath the cremation chimney*

The photo boards at Site 1 where each day hundreds of distraught relatives would visit searching for their missing loved ones amongst the photos

Site 1: some of the containers each holding between 60 and 80 bodies

*Me, Pecky and Gadge cooling off inside
a refrigerated container with all the bodies*

*Loading the bodies onto gurneys ready to begin the
identification process. The gurneys were pushed by Thai
army lads, some who had lost close relatives in the tsunami*

Site 2 rest area reminiscent of MASH

*Just entering a container to audit all of the bodies
to make sure they were all in their correct places*

The little one-eared bunny on the beach that completely caught me out. Even now I wish I'd brought him home

Me, Gorgeous George on my right, and Pecky on my left, on the way back from work. We smelled really bad!

THE CHILDREN

While working at Site 1, we learned of a group of children who had been rescued and taken to temporary accommodation nearby. We understood that these children had lost their relatives and homes. We decided as a group to go and visit them, and before going there, we had a whip-round to raise a bit of money for treats. We bought sweets and toys but nothing of any great help. We didn't really know what to buy, actually. We drove for ten minutes and arrived at a large tent at the side of a pond.

There was a great deal of noise and a lot of activity, and suddenly we were faced with thirty-two beautiful smiling faces, all looking at us with hope in their eyes.

In Thailand, there is a foundation called the Duang Prateep Foundation. Prateep is an amazing lady who is tiny in size but large in personality. As a young girl, she grew up realizing that to be successful as a female in Thailand, you needed to be educated. She raised money and paid her way through university. She then decided to do the same for other women from the slums of Bangkok. The Duang Prateep Foundation still helps females with their education. She also helps to educate people living in the slums to protect them against fire hazards and promote good health. Each year they send a travelling puppet theatre out into the remote villages of Thailand to educate villagers in a fun way with puppets against paedophilia, prostitution and drugs. *(Girls in these villages are sold by their parents to gangs in the cities to raise money for the other family members)*. Prateep, on hearing about the tsunami asked for someone to go straight to Phang Nga to round up any abandoned children.

One lady fitted the bill: Rotjana Phraesrithong. Rotjana grew up on a jungle farm outside Petchaburi in central Thailand to the west of Bangkok. She had a very simple but happy childhood and had no form of education until Prateep decided at the age of sixteen that Rotjana should be educated.

Prateep was a relative of Rotjana and knew that here was a girl with spirit and intelligence. Rotjana attended school unable to read or write in Thai or speak English but within a year was able to do all three and read and write in English.

This intelligent young girl had caught up rapidly and finished at university with qualifications. She then worked alongside Prateep mainly with the puppet theatre.

Later on, she had a partner and became pregnant with her daughter Ton Palm *(Palm tree)*. Following the tsunami, Rotjana immediately went over to Takua Pa with Ton Palm who at the time was an infant and began rescuing the kids. By the time I first met her, she had rescued the thirty-two children who were now looking at us with their big brown eyes.

Conditions in the tent were basic, and Rotjana

was working round the clock with local women, and an English woman called Allyson to make the tent a safe and loving environment for these thirty-two lost souls. We handed out the sweets and toys and each time received a gracious *'Thank you'* in Thai. In retrospect toys and sweets were probably the last thing they needed on a very long shopping list. I came away from the tent feeling humbled and overwhelmed with sadness. I was not a maternal woman; however, I could not get these thirty-two sets of bright eyes out of my head or the tireless efforts of this incredible lady, Khun Rotjana (Khun is a Thai term of respect for men and women). Before I left the tent, I obtained her details promising to keep in touch.

Very quickly our month in Thailand was coming to an end, but before I had even left the country, I was informed that a request had been put in for me to go back out with three others in May.

Our first-ever visit to the kids in the tent

The kids queuing up for sweets

Dishing out the sweets

BACK IN BLIGHTY

We boarded the plane in Bangkok and slept through most of the flight. I did not care if there was a nice diamond dealer sitting next to me on this journey. We arrived back into Heathrow and were ushered straight into the Heathrow special arrivals lounge for a hot debrief. All I can remember at the time was that the first person I saw on walking into the lounge was Lawrence Dallaglio nursing a broken ankle from his New Zealand Lions tour and thinking, wow he's gorgeous!

We were immediately ordered to take a week's leave, so after a good night's kip, I drove up to Skye for a week where I felt I was emerging from my bubble. After seeing the sights I had seen, and how the locals were just getting on with their lives despite all that had been lost, how having lost more than is humanly possible yet behave in such a peaceful and dignified manner, my world felt very artificial, and I felt I had changed. I did not want irrelevant things to matter to me anymore. They did not deserve to matter anymore. I was so lucky with my life, and I felt I should never complain about anything ever again.

After a week on Skye, I was pretty much ready to get back to work and more importantly, I had a plan. I wanted to raise money for Rotjana. My thoughts were constantly drifting back to this incredible lady who gave everything and wanted nothing. In the short time I had before going back out to Thailand for my second deployment, I had a great deal to sort out. Back to the daily life of *Specialist Search and Recovery*, sorting out budgets and annual leave, trying to decide which three officers to take back out with me in May and also how to raise a chunk of money for Rotjana.

In between all of this, we were summoned for health checks, individual psychological assessments and a team assessment at a posh country house in-between Oxford and Woodstock. We were told that we had to attend, none of us really wanted to go, but the offer of a decent lunch thrown in was too much to refuse.

The assessment was bizarre; we were a great team; we debriefed each day on-site in Thailand and looked after each other. In fact, I partnered everyone up so that everyone had a buddy to watch out for them. The lady taking the assessment or debrief, whatever you want to call it, somehow was expecting us to be shell-shocked, paranoid or withdrawn but we were all happy, we had worked hard and put our skills to great use, we had looked after each other and basically had a great but highly unusual time and here she was trying to draw out of us something that really did not exist.

I think she soon realized that we were more anxious about being late for dinner, gave up and thanked us for coming.

During that time I decided to run the West

Highland Way which was a distance of 96 miles from Glasgow to Fort William and then cycle the 106 miles from Fort William to my house on Skye via the Mallaig-Armadale ferry. It took me four days of running nearly 25 miles a day, then about six hours of cycling at the end. My efforts raised about £3000.

TOUR 2
SITE 2

By now, I was already in full planning mode to go back out to Thailand. This time, I was going out with three others: Nick Peck ('Pecky', my best mate and crewmate on the diving team); Steve Underhill ('Animal', a crazy ex-dog handler and just brilliant to hang out with); and George Tunnah ('Gorgeous George', who was simply a lovely guy to work with and great fun). They were all chosen, firstly, because they had all been out there on the first deployment and knew the ropes and secondly and most importantly, they were just good guys and so easy to get on with and work alongside.

We travelled out in May staying in a different hotel at Karon beach on the west coast of Phuket and working at Site 2. It was quite obvious that by now, things had been scaled down and that personnel had been reduced quite dramatically. Site 2 still had its seventy-two containers which were still mostly full of unidentified bodies. We were working with an inspector from Greater Manchester and three constables.

Our hours were the same as before, but because our travel time was shortened to about half an hour, we had a bit more downtime. We just had enough time each evening to get a swim in before the sun went down. Site 2 was still busy, there were still bodies awaiting the identification process, but more so we were helping with the release of them as more had been formally identified through this same process. Basically, once the *Identification Commission* approved the identification, a list of unique reference numbers was emailed through each evening, each number relating to a body that had been formally identified. This information was received into the office at Site 2 so that each body with the corresponding number could be brought up to a holding container just across from the office. First thing in the morning all the paperwork was checked against the unique reference number on the body, then the pathologists and dentists would conduct a final check of the body to ensure everything matched the details. Once they were satisfied, the bodies would be ready for release.

As I said before, if it were a Thai national, the relative would turn up with a piece of paper with the body reference number thereon. If it were a foreign national the embassy official for the country from where the victim originated would turn up. We noticed, however, that the locals were treated with total disrespect by the police officers from other nations working on-site. No names mentioned!

Having travelled for hours, the Thai relatives would be kept waiting at the main gate for many more hours before being brought in and made to stand and wait again in front of the mortuary doors where often a number of bodies were openly lying defrosting in the sun on their trolleys. It wasn't good. We were not impressed and very quickly got to work constructing a walkway around the back of the mortuaries directly into a tent where they could be dealt with in private. Even in Thailand, for us, it was still all about dignity and respect.

On one of the days, an Italian gentleman arrived on-site. I will never forget his story. He had been on a Christmas holiday to Thailand with his wife, who was disabled after breaking her back in a skiing accident. As a result, she could not use her legs and had to rely on a wheelchair. On the morning of the tsunami, he was pushing her alongside one of the beaches. As the wave came in, he desperately tried to outrun it pushing his wife ahead of him. Sadly, it caught up with him and his wife. The force of the water swept her away from him. He had searched for her for weeks before being informed that her body had been recovered. He was now at Site 2 to collect her body which had been identified by the plate fixed to her broken spine. This poor man clearly blamed himself and felt that it was his duty to take his wife back home rather than have her accompanied by an Italian embassy official. We listened to his story, tears in our eyes and each of us just gave him a hug. There were no words.

Halfway through this deployment, I arranged to go back to visit Rotjana and the kids with the money I had raised and so along with the other Brits we drove there one afternoon after work. It was still chaotic in the tent, Rotjana was still slaving away along with her helpers, and the kids were just shell-shocked kids, I guess.

I sat Rotjana down and asked her what was it she needed right now. She tentatively asked for a television. I asked her what else and she replied, "Musical instruments and a CD player," as the kids find music and dance very therapeutic.

I inquired if there was anything else, and she replied, "Rice, baby milk, and fans." I immediately got our driver Ted to run me to the Big C supermarket in Phuket where I purchased all of these items and more for Rotjana and arranged for them to be delivered the next day. I also managed to buy guitars, tambourines and recorders from a music shop in Phuket.

The next time I visited Rotjana before leaving Thailand, the place was chaotic with recorders blasting and guitars strumming, girls were dancing to music, and the little ones were huddled around the TV all the while being kept cool in the breeze of some big fans.

Before I left Thailand, I was informed that I would be coming back out in August on my own.

Soon we returned to the UK at Heathrow. This time there was no special lounge, and no debriefs and sadly no Lawrence Dallaglio. We were obviously deemed physically and mentally fit from the last time. I had to take another week off so headed off to Skye for some hard-earned rest and slowly emerged from my bubble again before heading back to work and normality. All the while, I was deciding how to raise more money.

This time it had to be the West Highland Way back-to-back with the Great Glen Way: 170 miles running from Glasgow to Fort William and then across to Inverness. I absolutely loved doing these long runs; it meant I could spend real quality time with my mum and dad. Throughout all of my mad long-distance adventures over the years they always immediately jumped at being my support crew, this was no exception, my dad felt part of the adventure and my mum just loved to know she was helping someone somehow. The only downside was the sore head each morning following an evening of beer and laughter. This run raised another £3000.

I knew that on the next deployment I would be on my own. I was happy with the travel and everything but would there be anyone to have a drink with or go to the gym with in the evening? Plus I really did not know who I would be working with. All I knew was that I would be the *Body Release Officer* at Site 2.

My mum and dad support crewing me
on one of my long-distance runs

Some of the items bought after my first charity run.
(Rotjana is in the right foreground)

Me and my dad on another fundraising run

On a 640-mile bike ride from the Isle of Skye to Marlow

The tent the kids called home

Daily activities to keep the kids occupied

THE FINAL TOUR
SITE 2

On arrival in Bangkok, I hitched a lift with some British police officers working in the admin offices and who were staying at the same hotel.

The next morning I was up and ready for work to discover my transport had not been arranged. Fortunately, I had the number of the transport company and Joey, the owner, sent me a driver, Arkhom who could speak very little English. Arkhom would be my driver for the whole month, and we actually got on like a house on fire. We became firm friends, and I still speak to him on the phone to this day and always use him whenever I am revisiting Thailand. I taught him some English, and he tried to teach me Thai. We got by and spent most mornings and evenings laughing at each other's feeble attempts at each other's language. Arkhom was really protective of me and was also so proud to be my driver. He was a true gentleman and invited me into his home to meet his lovely family, which was a real honour.

On arrival at Site 2, I noticed that it was much more overgrown, the jungle was reclaiming its rightful ground. In the early days, there would often be around two-hundred people working on-site, and so the wildlife and plants were kept at bay. Now there was me, five Aussie cops, two British pathologists and a handful of Thai soldiers plus the canteen staff. The wildlife was creeping back in, and nearly every day one of the Aussies would come in with a snake impaled on a knife — reminiscent of Crocodile Dundee.

Scorpions and spiders were turning up in paperwork, under seats and in any boots or clothing lying around, so everything had to be checked before sitting down or before picking stuff up. A large number of the bodies had by now also been released. There were still seventy-two containers, but most were half empty.

One of our first tasks was to consolidate all of the remaining bodies into containers closer to the mortuaries so that we were not walking for miles each time to fetch a body for release.

The Aussies were headed up by Detective Inspector Peter Baines who would be the site commander. He and I would be working out of the same office. He had worked at Site 1 in the very early days. The others were forensic cops, a dentist and two British pathologists, one of whom was called Tony Cullen, a truly lovely man who sadly passed away only a few years back. His son contacted me out of the blue, writing such a beautiful letter expressing how much Tony had enjoyed working with me and also to inform me that he had died. Such a sad loss.

We hit the ground running with barely a handover, and I immediately had to receive details of bodies to be released the next day. I had checked everything off with data on my computer and printed off a list which I handed to the Aussies, and they hunted down the bodies which were all placed in a defrosting holding container opposite the office. Overnight the bodies would thaw out so that they would be pliable enough for the experts to examine them. This was to confirm that the physical details matched those on the ID report. The body was then sealed up in a new bag awaiting collection. I would be informed when the relative or embassy official was to collect the respective body and right from the offset I insisted that there would be no more waiting at the gate, the person on security would bring the Thai relatives to a seating area under an open-sided canopy. There I would meet them and offer them cold drinks or the use of the toilet.

I had a Thai police interpreter with me who translated everything for me. I had learned to say hello, goodbye and thank you, but I also insisted that I learned to count in Thai. The reason for this was because the relatives turned up with an information sheet containing the unique reference number of their identified loved one, I had a body sealed in a bag with the same unique reference number. The least I could do was attempt to communicate with them; all be it in a very limited way. And they really appreciated it. Often the relatives would be totally distraught; this was their son, daughter, sister, brother after all and often had already attended the site to collect other relatives lost to the wave. They would be crying and I was very slow going through the numbers in broken Thai. This always had such a positive effect; they would often step in and correct me, breaking into a smile and definitely breaking down any barriers. I would then walk them around to the back of the release tent where their loved one would be lying in the sealed bag in a coffin. I would again go through the numbers on the bag in my very poor Thai. On a daily basis my heart would break at the sight of these poor souls coming to collect yet another family member. They simply dealt with everything in such a peaceful and dignified way. The Thais are quite timid and not really into hugging but every day I would wrap my arms around them and hug them as if their life depended on it. It did not matter, and they appreciated the fact that here was someone from thousands of miles away, from a different culture offering them comfort and who truly cared. Every day ended in tears for me as I tried to control my emotions but each time hopelessly failing. I would stand in front of the big fan situated in the release tent, it sprayed out cold water in a fine mist, and I would pretend that my tears were just the drops of water. At the end of four weeks, I didn't care what anyone thought. I cried with them and for them.

While in the tent, the relatives had access to incense sticks, candles, tissues and a Buddha so that they could pray or light a candle. I would give them time to open the coffin but not the body bag, that was one rule I adhered to. Often they would turn up with photos of their lost loved one, and I always had to explain through my interpreter that it was best that they remembered that person as he or she was on the photo because what was in the body bag no longer resembled that person. They would lay clean clothes in the coffin, sprinkle aromatic tea over the body and place personal items around it in readiness for the next life. Money for wealth and clothes to wear.

Being Buddhist they believed that the soul would move on. The final thing they did before sealing the coffin was to place a short piece of string with a knot at either end on the side of the coffin so that when the lid was down one end was hanging inside and the other end was hanging outside, the knots preventing it from being pulled out. It was explained that this provided a route to the outside world for the soul if it hadn't already left the body. The coffin was then taken away to a crematorium for cremation.

I found it incredibly moving, and peaceful watching how death was dealt with in the Buddhist way and by placing personal items with the body seemed to assist with the grieving process.

There were other Brits at the hotel I was staying at who were working in the admin offices in Phuket. Most of the time they seemed to swan around going to embassy parties or complaining that the air con had failed in their office all day forcing them to go back to the hotel and the pool to cool down. I would have loved to have them spend just one day with me at Site 2. They were totally oblivious to the fact that I was working on-site. During this time, I was the only operational Brit working out there. Most nights, I got back to the hotel, stripped off at the door, still forever embarrassed about the deathly stench lingering on my work clothes before calling laundry to come and deal with it all. I spent most nights in the gym, grabbing a bite to eat before crashing out completely.

The two British pathologists were staying along the coast at a different hotel, and the Aussies were staying right on the southern tip of Phuket so there was very little socialising to be had plus I was always exhausted. I managed a couple of nights out with the Aussies where we ended up dancing in a club in downtown Phuket called the Timber Hut, a real fire hazard. I was simply too tired. One morning I was up at 0445am for work, arrived at Site 2 to be met at about 0700 by the Aussies, clearly the worse for wear. They had got into bed at 0500, getting an hour's kip before coming to work. I pointed out to them that I had actually got up for work before they had got to bed, and now here they were!

I found this trip to be the most exhausting out of the three, mainly because of the raw emotion of grief I was being faced with all day every day. Halfway through this trip, I ended up at the Bangkok Hospital in Phuket late one evening suffering from severe stomach pains. I contacted a British police superintendent who was working in the offices at this time just to let someone know that I was going to the hospital in case something happened to me. He was at an embassy party and clearly didn't want to speak, didn't care who I was and was totally unaware that there was a British police officer out there working amongst the bodies on Site 2. It seemed to me that this crowd were just out for the parties and the social scene. In the end, I phoned my own superintendent in the UK and informed him exactly what was happening and very quickly word got round in Thailand what was happening. I immediately received a 'welfare' call from a female chief inspector offering her assistance. The hospital trip showed I had a small kidney stone which was treated immediately and fortunately no more pain. Tony, the pathologist, was very impressed with the standard of treatment I had received when I turned up for work the next morning feeling great again.

Halfway through the tour, I got Arkhom to drive me out to the tent and to see Rotjana. It was still chaotic, and Rotjana was working her socks off. I asked Rotjana what she really needed now, and the response was instant: a washing machine, washing powder, rice and baby milk. They had been washing the children's clothes in the pond, and the kids were developing skin rashes. Arkhom immediately drove me to Big C again where I purchased a big industrial washing machine (which only died in 2017), tubs of washing powder, sacks of rice and baby milk. It was delivered the next day.

On my last night in Thailand, I asked Arkhom to drive me to see the children. I sat with Rotjana, and we talked for hours. We had become good friends, and despite our cultural differences, we just got on so well. I asked her what she really wanted for the kids. She replied, "A proper home," and she then explained that these kids would otherwise be living in the tent until they were eighteen. I was shocked. After everything they had been through, one girl had lost seventeen members of her family, another had lost twenty-two and to then not have a proper home. This just wasn't right.

I left Thailand unable to really settle because of my last chat with Rotjana. Here was a woman who had given up her life to look after these poor kids. She deserved more than a tent for them.

On the last day in Thailand, I had been asked to travel over to Phi Phi Island to conduct a risk assessment to search all of the water-filled pools and ditches on the island. Phi Phi Island was hit really hard by the tsunami; over seventy percent of the buildings were destroyed, and 850 bodies had been recovered. An estimated 1,200 people are still missing. This island should have looked like paradise, it now resembled a complete disaster zone, and the smell of death and contaminated sewers filled the air even eight months after the event. The one main hotel was desperately trying to fill upper-level rooms but was surrounded by pools and ornamental lagoons filled with rancid water. I spent a day inspecting each pool trying to formulate a plan to search through these areas to eliminate the possibility of any more bodies. Some could be waded; however, the majority were too deep to wade and would need to be dived. On my journey back to the hotel, I pulled together a complete risk assessment to search each area and handed it over. My job was now done.

There was a possibility that I would get asked to put together a team to come back out to search these areas, but this did not materialize. I understand that the Thai authorities could not wait, they were desperate to get Phi Phi rebuilt and filled with tourists again and searched the pools as best they could before filling them in. I have never been convinced that the pools were searched properly, some were as large as football pitches. I love Thailand, I have returned to Phi Phi but would never stay there.

This was my last visit to see Rotjana and the kids before finishing work and returning to the UK. The white-haired chap on the right is Tony Cullen the forensic Pathologist

This was the moment when I asked Rotjana what she wanted for the kids, and she replied 'a proper home'

HANDS ACROSS
THE WATER UK

I returned to the UK absolutely drained following my work as the *Body Release Officer.* The mental toll of dealing with so much raw emotion all day every day for a month had exhausted me, and I was glad to ease out of my bubble up on Skye.

A request was sent to my chief constable from Tony the British pathologist asking if I could be released to work on Site 2 with him in November. I was extremely flattered by this very kind request, but by now my life had been put on hold for almost a year, and Ian and I desperately needed a holiday, on top of that I still had a team to run, so I politely turned down the request.

Normality back at work was instant, sat in my office and suddenly I would hear, *"Sarge!"*

"What Clarky?"

"Tell Little Legs *(Martin, because he's got short legs)* to stop looking at me with his eyes."

"Martin, behave. Clarky, stop telling tales."

I loved these guys and their silliness.Within five minutes of being back in the office, it felt as if I had never been away. The same old crazy gang, jobs filling the board needing to be dealt with and recruiting for new team members.

This was one aspect of my job that I equally enjoyed and hated. In total contrast to when I applied to become a diver where I had been thrown into hazardous waters to gain experience. These days our aptitude tests lasted a week, testing physical fitness, swimming fitness, a diving medical, swimming pool diving tests, a confined space test and open water diving tests. It was pretty much full-on and took a great deal of planning.

At the end of all the tests was the formal interview where all the scores from each test were then added up, and whoever came out on top was selected. I loved the week of testing but hated having to inform those not successful of the result. Most applicants were very capable but didn't make it through due to the tiniest error or failing. Some of the lesser-able could not understand that a twelve-minute cut off time was there for a reason and the fact that they finish the swim in twelve minutes ten seconds meant that they had failed the test or as they swam the first length of sixteen they started swimming doggy paddle.

One of my other roles was a national one. After I was promoted back onto the team, I was asked to be part of a small committee tasked by the *Association of Chief Police Officers (Marine and Diving)* and the *Health and Safety Executive* to look at the *Police Diving Manual* which was our bible and completely bring it up to date. At the time it was based on the *Royal Navy Diving Manual,* some of which is still relevant but most of which is outdated. The manual is a thick one with a great deal of content. It took hours of work and meetings to get it to the manual it is today and is something that I was very proud to have worked on and contributed to and for the last four years of my career, I became secretary of this group. As a result of the new *Police Diving Manual, the Diving Aptitude* test was so much safer.

With all this going on, the team were working flat out, and I was working flat out, but during every moment of downtime, my mind was constantly thinking about a dear Thai lady who was now my very dear friend. We spoke regularly on the phone, laughed and cried a lot against the background of thirty-two noisy children who always were put onto the phone to say hello to Khun Gill. It broke my heart. I knew that I could not sit there, acting as if they did not exist. I spoke with Ian, my mum and dad and close friends and with their support decided that I was in a position to do something about it. I contacted Rotjana and told her that I wanted to build her a home for the children. I needed her to get plans drawn up and a cost. Sometime around the middle of September 2005, Rotjana emailed me with the plans. A new home was going to cost £50,000. I can remember thinking, can I really do this, I can raise £3000 but can I take the next big step? I knew what the answer was and knew that I would give it a very good attempt.

As I have previously mentioned, I always love a challenge.

I immediately started the ball rolling. I approached my bosses in the hope that TVP would support me. TVP was brilliant; not only did they contribute thousands to my fundraising; they fully supported me travelling around the country talking to groups and organisations to raise awareness and money. And after all, it also looked good for them to show off one of their officers. I really did not mind so long as I raised that £50,000 for Rotjana and the kids. It was at this stage that I fully understood the enormity of my mission and that I would need to register a charity, and I needed to drum up support. I contacted my colleague from Thailand, Peter and asked whether he would sponsor me, his immediate response was, "This is exactly what I need, I can do better than that." He decided to start a charity in Australia. The name of mine would be *Hands Across the Water UK*, his the same but *Australia* at the end. Not to get confused, the two charities were not linked in any way.

I immediately started on a round of talks to Rotary clubs, round-tables, women's institutes, police groups, hospitals and schools, you name it. In some cases, my evenings gathered pounds, on others hundreds of pounds. It did not matter as every penny counted. My total was beginning to add up, and my roadshow got momentum.

I then received a call from the chairman of Marlow Football Club who I had known while working at Marlow police station in the early eighties. He asked if I could attend the club on the following Wednesday night to receive a donation. For some reason, I thought it would be a big whisky bottle full of coins. When I arrived there, I was handed a cheque for £16000. I was absolutely speechless. The club had decided to fundraise following the tsunami but did not know where to donate the money and then by chance one of the members had seen a photo of me in one of the local papers and read an interview about my work in Thailand. *Local girl, local policewoman* — perfect!

I also received an email out of the blue from a lady called Yvette in York. Her daughter Sarah was on holiday on Phi Phi Island with her boyfriend when the tsunami hit the island. They were caught by the wave — they are two of the British victims whose bodies have never been recovered. Yvette and her husband Paul had been handed a large amount of money to donate to a charity to help tsunami victims in memory of Sarah. Paul had trawled the internet for such a charity, but nothing caught his eye until he found mine. Yvette sent an email and said the money is yours as long as you promise to give a talk to Sarah's old school in York and a college in Warrington where one of her ex-tutors now worked. I immediately replied yes and then sat and cried my eyes out at the overwhelming and selfless generosity of this couple whose lives had been changed forever.

Within a couple of months of having my charity registered, we smashed through the £50,000 target and continued up and beyond. It was simply the best feeling in the world to phone Rotjana up to tell her that she could now start building her home for the kids. She cried. I cried.

Over the coming months, the money just rolled in. I was giving presentations to two or three groups a week, and family and friends were running marathons, swimathons, you name it to raise just that little bit more.

I then learned that the Thai treasury had heard what was happening and had agreed to match the £50,000 so Rotjana could build an even bigger home.

In August 2006 Ian and I were guests at the official opening of the Baan Than Namchai Orphanage in Takua Pa where all thirty-two children were the stars of the show. The orphanage was built in the village from where most of the children had lived before. Rotjana explained that it was good for the orphans to grow up surrounded by survivors who were family friends or school friends. The orphanage was to become the hub for the village. Village children would be included in all activities, as far as Rotjana was concerned they were all victims, they may well be living at home, but they had also lost a parent, a brother, sister, aunt or uncle. She did not want the village kids to resent the orphanage kids who were getting a great deal of attention and gifts. She shared it equally. Women from the village were already working for Rotjana and were now receiving recognized training to look after them.

The day was hot, the atmosphere was exciting and happy, the kids were beautiful, and Rotjana was shining. It was an absolute joy to see her so happy. She had got her home for the kids at last. The tent was now a distant memory. The building was painted in green, and the garden walls were painted with cartoon characters.

The garden was full of playground equipment, and each child had a bunk bed and wardrobe. Each child took so much pride in showing you their bed and wardrobe; to them, it was a palace. One of the bedrooms had a plaque above the door *'Sarah's Room'* in memory of a young lady whose death has created so much life and hope for others.

The new home at Baan Than Namchai

The opening ceremony

Presenting Rotjana with the keys to a new vehicle

BRIGHT AND DARK DAYS

I arrived back home to a round of further talk requests mainly from groups wanting updates and to see photos of the new home which kicked off more money being raised.

Over the next couple of years, Ian and I visited Thailand on a couple of occasions.

HATWUK purchased a minibus and a car and planted a rubber plantation which would generate further income for the home once the trees were mature.

In 2007 I was informed that I had been nominated for the Thames Valley Police Individual Shrievalty Award. The three high sheriffs of Oxfordshire, Berkshire and Buckinghamshire look at the nominations and decide who in their opinion, deserved the individual award and who should be awarded the team award. They voted that I should be presented with the individual award for leading the way for policewomen in specialized roles, my work on the national committee for enhancing the safety of police divers, developing the dignity in death procedures recovering dead bodies, the mini-major disasters I had dealt with, my work on the tsunami and my charity work.

On Sunday, 12th March, 2007, my mum and dad drove from Skye to Marlow in readiness for the ceremony which was to be held on Thursday, 15th. My dad was on top form and was dragging me out to the *'Southern Office'* (the local pub) every night for a few beers, (the Stein Inn on Waternish, Skye was his *'Northern Office'*). I noticed that he brought with him a list of about twenty friends from Oxford whom he wanted to visit. By the Wednesday he had achieved this and seemed really content. Ian flew down on the Wednesday to also attend the ceremony.

Just prior to leaving for the ceremony, my dad stopped me and asked if he looked okay with the tie he was wearing. I remember looking into his kind blue eyes saying, "Dad, you look lovely."

On the drive over, he asked on which table they would be seated. I informed them that we were all together and that the Chief Constable, Sara Thornton, had specifically asked me if she could sit next to my dad. My dad, who was always so modest, could not understand why she would want to do that.

I was seated at a large round table. The silverware and white linen—all beautifully arranged. I glanced across to my dad; he looked amazing. 76-years-old, pure white hair and not a wrinkle on his face. What was he on? I wanted some of it. He looked so smart, and he caught my eye and winked at me. There was so much pride in those bright blue eyes and in that moment I realized just how much all of this meant to him. I could not have wished for more and just knew that he would be reliving this occasion with his many friends in the pub in the weeks ahead. I was then called up to the front of the stage to be presented with my award.

The high sheriff of Berkshire, John Miller, was to read out my citation and present my award but decided instead to read out my whole career history. I was overwhelmed and very flattered with this nomination. Ian and my mum and dad were sat just a short distance away, all with big smiles on their faces. I felt immensely proud at receiving the award but felt I was also accepting it on behalf of Ian, my mum and dad and my team, all who have supported me throughout. My team deserved untold awards for their constant efforts and loyalty, not just to me but to the police service in general.

Following the presentations, we were served a lovely meal, and it was brilliant to see my dad laughing and joking with his new best friend, Sara.

On the Sunday following the ceremony, Ian and I flew off to the Arctic Circle in Finland for some cross-country skiing while my mum and dad drove back up to Skye.

At about 8.10am on Tuesday, 20th March, my mobile rang to show Madeline's name flash up on the screen. She and Graham lived about half a mile away from us on Skye.

"Hi, Madeline."

"Gill, I thought you needed to know, I am with your mum and dad. We think your dad is having a heart attack and they are working on him now, I am really sorry to break this news to you."

I could not breathe; my world stopped moving.

Within minutes that felt like a lifetime came the words, "Gill, I'm so sorry, he has died."

Ian was brilliant and arranged emergency flights to Helsinki and then back to Heathrow. Our car was parked at Gatwick, so Pecky was waiting for us at Heathrow ready to drive to Gatwick. We then drove all the way up through the night arriving on Skye early on the most stunning pink sunrise to say my goodbye to my dad now lying in the undertakers in Portree.

My best friend, the man who shared all of my adventures, the man who loved people and whom they loved in return. No more. I had suffered physical pain before, but I had truly never experienced emotional pain in my heart. It felt like it would never go away, and it hurt so bad. I was also deeply concerned about my mum, who was always so reliant on my dad. She was pretty amazing and initially handled everything better than me and better than I ever thought she would. She had lost her husband of over fifty years. At his funeral we placed his favourite clothes into his coffin alongside a book I had bought him, reading glasses, money, an old warrant card of mine (in case he got into trouble up there) and hanging from the side of his coffin, a piece of string with a knot at the end.

Everyone who knew my dad was devastated. I understand that Sara Thornton was really upset to learn that the lovely man she had been teasing the week before had died. On reflection, I think he knew that something wasn't right and visiting all of his old friends in Oxford was like a last goodbye. I was so relieved that I had spent the most amazing week with him in Marlow and that he was there for my presentation.

TVP supported me so much during this time for which I am eternally grateful.

As they say, life must go on, and I was soon back into work and more presentations to groups. The pain in my heart eased but will always be there for a man I truly loved unconditionally: my dad.

Within weeks of the funeral, my mum bravely support-crewed me with friends while I ran the West Highland Way again to raise more money. I've still got my t-shirt: *'Running for my dad'*.

During the summer of 2008, an official letter arrived at the flat in Marlow. I honestly thought that it was a speeding ticket from driving a bit too fast on a journey home from work a few weeks before. I threw it to one side and forgot about it. I remembered it five days later and thought I had better take a look.

It was a letter from Her Majesty the Queen inviting me to Buckingham Palace to receive the Queen's Police Medal for my achievements. I nearly fell over. I certainly dropped the letter. I was in a complete mess when I phoned Ian who went absolutely mad and no doubt was on the phone to everyone once I had hung up.

In December 2008, together with Ian, my mum and Ian's mum, I attended Buckingham Palace.

TVP laid on the whole works with the chief's car and chauffeur who took us for a tour and then had arranged passes into the inner courtyard of the palace. As we drove through the gates, the security guard mentioned that he had just checked in Joe Cocker who was to receive an OBE for his contribution to music. Joe was and still is one of my favorite singers and so to be there at the same time was truly the icing on the cake.

Once inside, I was separated from the others and had to go into a large and incredibly ornate hall where all of the other recipients were to be addressed before being called forward to receive their respective awards. Ian and the mums were ushered into the ballroom where they took their seats. I entered the hall bedecked with the biggest Christmas trees I had ever seen indoors.

The room was packed full of people all making polite chit-chat. I noticed Ryan Giggs wandering about, and then I saw him, Joe, stood on his own at the back of the room. I thought, 'Here goes, if I don't say anything, I will be kicking myself for the rest of my life.' I walked over to him and just said, "Hello, Joe, you don't know me, but I've always loved your music and just want to congratulate you on your award." He was brilliant, what a lovely, funny guy and we spent the rest of the time before being called forward chatting about anything and everything. I still have my photo of us together afterwards. We were then given our briefing explaining what to do and what to say and more importantly, when to know to walk away. It would be Prince Charles who would be running the show today.

"Police Sergeant Gill Williams, for her contribution to police work and charity!"

My heart was pounding as I walked across in front of probably three-hundred guests. I stopped in front of Prince Charles, turned left towards him, stepped forward two paces, semi-curtseyed and stopped. My jaw nearly dropped. Prince Charles has the most amazing twinkling blue eyes, and I remember thinking, 'You are really quite gorgeous.' I can remember him asking if I was still diving. I had actually worked alongside him on a number of jobs over the years and often in Windsor. We talked diving; we talked about the Mary Rose, I invited him to come for a dive in the Thames at Windsor from his garden, and we had a laugh. He pinned my medal to my tunic, and I realized that the signal to leave had just been given. I thanked him very much, made a complete hash of my semi-curtsey and walked off.

I found Ian and the mums and filled them in on my chat with Joe before introducing them to him and getting my photo taken. *Oh,* and I also told them of my conversation with Prince Charles. It was an incredible day but bittersweet because I know that my dad would have loved it.

Over my final few years in the police, the team had to attend a course in Portland Down where we were qualified as the team to use in the event of a chemical, biological, radioactive or nuclear attack. We were kitted out to enter a hot zone and help to identify bodies. This was now scary stuff, and one skill in our toolbox of skills that I hoped and prayed would never get used.

As a direct result of the tsunami, the UK police devised a *Victim Identification* course to be run at Dundee University so that in the event of another major disaster every team would be working to the same standards, the same system and same kit. We were so lucky to have had a chief who had fully supported us with the right kit, equipment and training. We handed over to Devon and Cornwall constabulary teams after our first deployment and had to leave them some of our kit.

The course was amazing and was run by Professor Sue Black, the most incredible woman to listen to. She was a forensic anthropologist, her time spent looking at bones to discover who that person was and what had killed them. She later appeared on a weekly TV show where she was provided with a skull or other human remains and through intense research and expertise would provide either a description of this person or cause of death. She was fascinating and inspirational. I could have listened to her for hours. I can remember arriving in the lecture theatre on day one of the course to receive the course introduction from the Metropolitan Police bosses who had facilitated it all.

During the intro, I noticed a quite scruffy ginger-haired woman walk in and sit down. I am ashamed to say I thought she was a lab assistant due to her manner and expression. This was Sue Black, totally understated, and absolutely mesmerizing. We were given our own cadavers to practice on for whole the week. These were bodies donated for medical science. Our first lesson from Sue was all about total respect for the dead and the fact that they were to be treated with the same dignity afforded to a living being. This was a woman after my own heart. She explained in no uncertain terms that if she caught anyone joking or messing about with their cadaver, they would immediately be sent home. For me, this week was not long enough as Sue was such a brilliant teacher and taught me so much. As part of the course, we had to write a thesis on a disaster, any disaster, describe it in detail, including lessons learned. Mine was all about the Lambourne air disaster high up on the Downs all those years before. I was awarded a first.

UK police now had a *National Victim Identification Team* ready to spring into action anywhere in the world.

Receiving the Individual Shrievalty Award from the High Sheriff of Berkshire, John Miller

The last picture with my dad

Me and my mum

*Being awarded the Queen's Police Medal
by HRH Prince Charles*

With my medal

With Ian and our mums

With my mate Joe Cocker

LIFE GOES ON

In 2007 we discovered that Rotjana had developed breast cancer and as a result had to undergo a double mastectomy.

Rotjana suffered dreadfully as a result of the treatment, both physically and mentally. Her thick black hair fell out, and she took to wearing an array of hats to cover up her bald head. A number of the teenage girls at the home shaved their heads so that Rotjana did not feel different. I can remember being there at the time seeing so many pretty bald-headed girls with Rotjana, all wearing their baldness with pride in support of their mum.

Rotjana eventually made a full recovery enabling her to once again run around with the kids who only knew her as their mum. It was a tough time for Rotjana, but her faith and spirit pulled her through. I lived in constant awe of her, not only was she recovering from a life-changing illness, but through it all, her love and commitment for the children never once faltered even during her darkest days.

I received a phone call from Rotjana one day shortly after her treatment had been completed. She asked whether I could buy her some new prosthetic boobs. Rotjana had decided to take a shower in her room, leaving her prosthetic boobies on the side. One of the little girls, a toddler was playing on the bed. Rotjana emerged from the shower to see the toddler chewing away at one of the boobies. There was only half a boobie left. The child was taken to the doctors but suffered no serious consequences; however, Rotjana was a little lopsided for a short while until I could get her new boobies! On another occasion, Rotjana had taken all of the kids swimming and while splashing about with them heard, *"Mama!!! Mama!!!* your boobies are floating,"* somehow they had escaped her costume for a swim of their own.

Despite terrible scars caused by the treatment, Rotjana always lived life to the full never letting the disfigurement of the operation get her down. However, it was always a constant reminder.

Over the years, the number of children at the home grew from thirty-two to forty-eight and very soon became sixty-four. The old home that had been built was beginning to become cramped for space.

Peter from Australia was now flying high with his charity and as a result, constructed a second building next to the first one.

In 2009, Ian and I were invited to participate in a 500-mile charity bike ride across Thailand with a group of Australians, cycling from Bangkok to Baan Than Namchai for the official opening of the second building. These two impressive buildings now housed the girls in one and boys in the other. There was also a large communal hall and dining room. The home was now a central focal point of the village; children from the home could meet and play with children from the village. Adults from the village either worked there or attended keep fit classes run by locals. I will never forget cycling along the road for the last mile surrounded by most of the kids on bikes and being greeted by Rotjana and so much noise from local musicians.

Rotjana insisted that every child at the home had to abide by the rules laid down there, these included respect for each other, working hard at school and also at the home. Their day starts at 0500 where all the children attend an exercise class, carry out chores and eat breakfast before being bussed to school. They finish school early, so have playtime, chores and tea. Each evening finishes with a chat and Buddhist prayers before going to bed. During school holidays Rotjana tried to get children with surviving family members to go and stay with them. She insisted that they never forgot their roots and maintained family links wherever possible.

For those without anyone, lessons in traditional rice-growing and Thai culture were the order of the day often with the kids up to their waists planting rice in mini paddy fields.

RETIREMENT

On January 20th, 2010, I completed my thirty years service with the police. From midnight I would be a civilian. I have been asked so many times do I miss my work. I can honestly say it was the smoothest transition from doing a job I absolutely loved, to doing what the heck I like. I love retirement and would recommend it to anyone.

Prior to retiring, I was asked to reconsider my decision to leave as I had already completed a great deal of planning and searching for the 2012 London Olympics. Part of which was at Dorney Lake near Windsor for the rowing and race canoeing. I can honestly say I was not even tempted. My mind was already looking forward to my new life up on Skye.

After retirement, we hosted a number of visits from the children in Thailand to Skye. They absolutely loved to come over. Rotjana even more so. She always enjoyed the months leading up to a trip over because the children behaved so well in the hope that they would get chosen to come. She would always spend time at the grave with my dad and would get the kids to sing Que Sera, which never failed to open the flood gates. The weather always seemed to be so cold whenever they came and so they would end up wearing all of mine and Ian's clothes just to keep themselves warm.

On their first visit, I made all of the bedrooms in the house up ready. All eight of them slept in one room! Ever since I've known what to do. They just crash out together. The people on Skye absolutely love the kids coming over and would fill the village hall to meet them, hear them sing and watch them dance. The Skye people have always been so generous in their support of the charity and are responsible for donating thousands of pounds over the years. I think the main reason for this is that they regularly got to meet the children that they had donated money for and everyone just fell in love with Rotjana. Our house would be in absolute chaos, kids everywhere and our Rhumdog chasing around after them. But it was always lovely chaos. After they left, we would sit there in the silence with heavy hearts missing the noise and laughter.

On one occasion, they specifically wanted to play in the snow. I was driving them down to Glasgow so thought that there would still be a bit up on the Nevis Range at Fort William even in May. I wrapped them all up warm and took them up in the gondola. I advised them not to roll in the snow as it was very cold. "Khun Gill, don't worry, we okay," was the reply. Fortunately, there was one solitary patch of snow just along from the top gondola station about half the size of a football pitch. They rolled and rolled and dumped snow and threw snow for about half an hour before I heard, "Khun Gill, we are soooooo cold!!!" I got them down quickly and into the warm. They had the time of their lives. And ever since every child who has come over has asked to play in the snow.

*The kids in freezing wet weather
at Dunvegan Castle on Skye*

The kids at Waternish Hall learning Bolly dancing

Please don't roll in the snow; you'll get cold—too late.
The highlight of their trip

HOME LIFE

Over the last few years, the charity has raised around £200,000 thanks to the generosity of friends and family and also to the many people that I have never met but who have supported us. We have also built a quiet room for the younger kids, completely rebuilt the music room for the band and bought new instruments, planted more rubber trees, repaired vehicles, treated the kids to trips and helped to fund the schooling needs of ten of the children. We have built a hydroponics unit where vegetables are grown to feed the kids, any excess is sold at market and in November 2017 replaced the original washing machine.

One young boy who visited called Gon was sixteen when he first came to Skye. When the tsunami hit his village, his mum and dad survived, but his mum was heavily pregnant at the time with his younger sister Nook. She was carried along with the wave and ingested the contaminated water into her lungs and stomach. Shortly after giving birth to Nook she passed away. As is often the case in Thailand, men tend to remarry very quickly and the new partner rejects children from the previous marriage. Shortly after his wife's death, Gon's dad remarried. Gon and Nook were rejected and abandoned at the orphanage where they have lived ever since. Gon is the most talented of musicians, he can pick up any instrument and play it. He is a brilliant guitarist and drummer and also very good on the flute. On leaving school, he wished to study music at university and is now in his fourth year of studies to become a drummer.

HATWUK have funded his education. Gon's dream is to return to the orphanage to teach music. On his last visit to Skye, Gon asked if he could call us his mum and dad. It was a moment when you realise that you are doing something right, and now when we speak, it always starts with, "Mum, how are you?"

Normally there are now around one-hundred children at the orphanage. The tsunami children are all grown up, most are either at or getting ready to start at university. Game was a 12-year-old boy when I first met him in the tent. He is now 28-years-old and has been to university and achieved a law degree and has a very bright future.

The non-tsunami orphans come from all walks of life. Their parents are in prison, they have been abused by parents and grandparents, parents have died, you name it, but they are welcomed with open arms into the security of Baan Than Namchai. Rotjana always said that she wished her arms were long enough to wrap around all of the children at once. I called her one day, and immediately she said, "Khun Gill, a 15-day-old baby boy has just been brought in, he was found in a rubbish bin and has no name. What can we call him?" I immediately replied, "Call him, Skye." Skye now is a healthy and cheeky 6-year-old.

Three years ago I stayed at the orphanage for three weeks. As I was leaving to drive to Phuket airport for my flight home, Rotjana insisted on accompanying me for the journey. Skye who was a toddler at the time also wanted to come. As Rotjana lifted him into the van she immediately groaned and said in Thai, "Skye you have pooped your pants, you smell. You are not coming with poop in your pants." She called one of the staff and asked them to take him to get changed. Skye by now was getting angry and said, "But mama, I have not pooped my pants; it was only a little gas." The smart 2-year-old was removed from the van!

Other stories include the two sisters aged six and two abandoned under the floors of a luxury hotel living in pools of water. The older sister fed them both from the scraps of food falling from the hotel. They are both normal happy girls now with a bright future ahead of them.

Ton Nam was abandoned at the home by his mother at just fifteen days old. Prior to his birth, his mother contacted Rotjana and explained that if Rotjana did not take care of her baby after it was born, she would have it aborted. Ton Nam now is a beautiful and happy little boy and a brilliant footballer.

Tiger is now twelve. He was first brought to the orphanage when he was five and was a nicotine addict, his only words were to ask for cigarettes. He had been abused by his stepfather who was a drug addict. He still has scars on his arms, legs and back. He has learning difficulties but attends a special school that helps him develop his talent for art and music. Without a doubt, this little boy would have died at the hands of his stepfather had he not come to Baan Than Namchai. And so it goes on, child after child each with their own horror story but now in the safe haven called Baan Than Namchai.

Following the tsunami, there were 370 victims recovered but not identified. This was because either whole families had been wiped out, they were alone in the world, or they were Burmese workers, working in Thailand illegally. Because of the regime in Burma at the time families there would have been too frightened to report them as missing due to possible repercussions from the Burmese authorities. These 370 victims are now buried at the *Tsunami Victims Cemetery* just outside Khao Lak. All the bodies are sealed in lead coffins, and their headstones consist of a metal plaque with the unique reference number engraved thereon. There is still a police post opposite the main entrance with all of the documentation relating to each victim in the hope that one day someone will come forward to reclaim their long lost loved one. Sadly, for most of the year, the cemetery is overgrown, but just before Boxing Day each year, Rotjana insists that every child goes to the cemetery, cuts the grass and tidies it all up so that it always looks smart for Boxing Day. She tells each child it is their duty because if it had not been for the tsunami, they would not be where they are now.

Ton Nam

Tiger

Phapet

Gon and Nook

Skye and Captain

Me and Tiger

Rotjana and Skye

Ton Nam: I taught him to swim front crawl
without armbands

LIFE DOES NOT GO ON

In 2016 while I was staying at the orphanage, Rotjana was complaining of pain in her hip. At the time the doctors found she had a kidney infection which may have contributed to the pain. However, the pain did not get better and in fact, became much worse. The year before, Allyson, the English lady who was Rotjana's friend and sister at the orphanage, developed a brain tumour, rapidly deteriorated and died back home in Ribchester in Lancashire.

Rotjana, Game and two others came over to me, and we drove down to the hospital for a last visit. It was heartbreaking to see. Allyson had been Rotjana's right-hand woman at the orphanage right from day one. She was also an amazing lady and had visited my house on Skye with the kids. Allyson sadly passed away within a few weeks, and I know that Rotjana never really got over her loss.

Rotjana came back over with Gon and some of the other children to attend the funeral with Gon playing the flute and the children singing. It was so moving to witness a fusion of Church of England and Buddhism at the funeral, and I have to say it worked really well.

By 2016 it was confirmed that Rotjana had developed secondary cancer in the bones of her hip. This was devastating news and difficult to understand why such a kind wise woman should have to suffer a second time. Wasn't once enough?

She came to Skye during this time using a stick and put on a brave face, but you could tell that she was in so much pain and was quite exhausted.

During this time, my dear mum was now living in a wonderful nursing home in Portree. She had developed vascular dementia, and it was so upsetting to watch this bright, cheerful lady reduced to a skeletal old woman filled with paranoia and fear. In a way I wish she had developed full-blown dementia leaving her oblivious to what was happening. Unfortunately, she still had many lucid moments where she was filled with the terror of what was happening to her. What can you say or do?

During her final two weeks, she stopped eating and drinking and lay sleeping and listening. I sat for hours every day, talking, showing her old photos and more importantly thanking her for being the best mum anyone could have wished for, for her support and encouragement to me throughout my childhood and career and also being my friend. I spoke about all my crazy long-distance challenges with her and my dad, which were such happy times. I was there till her last breath where I lay with my face next to hers telling her it was okay and she was going to be with dad again. She looked straight at me and died in my arms, and I was heartbroken again with that familiar pain of grief and loss in my heart.

At her funeral, inside her coffin, she had her favourite clothes, reading glasses, a book, a cuddly toy, money and another strange piece of string hanging out of the side of her coffin with a knot on the end. I have been so lucky to have parents who were also my friends.

By July 2017 it was clear that despite her treatment things were not improving, so Ian and I travelled out to Thailand for ten days to be with Rotjana. She was still mobile but only just and was still living in the hope that by some miracle, her body would respond to treatment. I attended the cancer hospital with her to speak with her surgeon Dr Phissit who agreed to try a different treatment for her. A very dear mutual friend, Kay Spencer from Australia had spoken with an oncologist who agreed to speak with Dr Phissit to discuss a newer treatment. I connected the two doctors in the hope that something could be done. Dr Phissit changed her treatment, and we spent weeks waiting to see if there was any improvement. By September Rotjana had deteriorated again, so I flew back out there for another ten days, I spent most of my time walking slowly around the garden of Baan Than Namchai with Rotjana in a wheelchair and attending hospital for more tests. We talked for hours and prayed with the monks at the local temple. When I came to say goodbye, Rotjana clung to me as if this would be the last time. It was so incredibly moving. I was filled with so much anger and frustration. I could not understand why she was suffering so much. She did not deserve it.

At the end of November, I went out again for another ten days. Things were getting desperate. Every day I would sit on the side of Rotjana's bed, just holding her hand or stroking her head. During the moments when she was awake and not sleepy from the influence of the many painkillers, we talked about her life, where she told me about growing up in Petchaburi. She also recorded a message for the children to be played after she had died.

Rotjana was completely exhausted, she was suffering incredible pain most of the time, and she was ready to die. Despite the intense pain and discomfort, whenever a child came into the room, Rotjana would open her arms to hug them. Even at this late stage, her only thoughts were for the children. Through our many chats, she admitted feeling angry and frustrated because all she still wanted was to play with the kids as she used to. She would often lie there so ill but still nursing a baby in her arms. She never stopped loving those kids. She had been afraid of dying but now accepted the inevitable. We prayed a lot. The monks came and prayed a lot. The staff and children prayed a lot. Rotjana also asked me to speak with the staff and then the children to explain to them what was going to happen. Up until this point everybody at the orphanage still held on to a glimmer of hope. Rotjana's lovely mum who I had grown to love and admire over the last couple of years would constantly hold on to me asking why. I had no answers. I, first of all, spoke with Rotjana's mum and Ton Palm, her daughter. They both knew and understood that time was running out fast. I told them to talk to her and to tell her what was in their hearts. And even at the end when they thought she was gone, to keep talking to her. The hearing is the last sense to go.

I then spoke with the staff, many I had known from the days in the tent. I sadly informed them that there was no hope, that Rotjana was going to die and it was probably going to be soon. I asked them to keep everything running for the sake of the children, to put the children first.

I then spoke with the children, all 102 of them who sat there on the floor, big brown eyes shining up from their innocent young faces, from toddlers to teenagers. This was harder than I ever imagined, telling 102 children that their mum was going to die soon. The lady who rescued them, gave them more love than they had ever known, who gave them security and hope for a bright future. I managed to keep it together until Phapet caught my eye and he smiled at me, and then I sort of lost it too. Phapet is just the most amazing young man who came to the orphanage with his brother and sister after his parents could not afford to look after them properly. He has a loving relationship with them and sees them often. And he has the wisdom and aura of someone much older. The smile on his handsome young face was just too much. He, who was so young and had been through so much, walked over and gave me a hug. Surely it should have been the other way round.

I left Thailand on this occasion knowing that I would never see Rotjana again, to laugh, joke, cry, gossip, sing and dance. In the early hours on the morning of Christmas Eve, Game called to inform me that Rotjana had passed away at the hospital. She was admitted a few days earlier, was delirious most of the time with drugs; however, earlier that morning she called Ton Palm, her mum and a few other relatives to her side. She told them what was in her heart, removed her oxygen mask, which was keeping her alive and died peacefully. She died on her terms, killing herself rather than being dictated to by the cancer.

There literally was an outpouring of grief from across the planet from people that had met Rotjana. She never realized just how important she was, not only saving the lives of so many children but bringing together so many strangers. She had touched so many hearts. Her body lay for a few days at her local temple right next door to where the tent had first been erected before moving her to the temple in Petchaburi where she grew up. Over a thousand people attended her funeral.

I didn't go to the funeral. Instead, Ian and I flew out to Thailand at the beginning of April for the memorial to commemorate the 100th day since her death. We all had to wear white. The monks all chanted and prayed and a bronze bust was uncovered revealing Rotjana carved from the metal. I gave a speech along with Peter and Kay but spent most of the day sitting with Rotjana's family who greeted me warmly as if I was part of their family. Strangely, the whole time I was there, it felt as if Rotjana was still there, you could really feel her presence. I guess her spirit was so strong, her heart so huge, the orphanage was Rotjana, and she was the orphanage.

I truly miss my friend and sister, from opposite ends of the Earth. Culturally opposite we just hit it off and loved each other. I have never met anyone who can or has equalled her with her wisdom, fairness and humanity. She truly was an angel, and the only explanation I can come up with for her death is because God or Buddha wanted her for himself because he has more work for her. The world is a darker place without her.

With my mum and dad celebrating New Year in 2005

My lovely mum shortly before she died

Rotjana: she became a nun for one month during August before she died. She hoped that by giving herself to Buddha it might provide a miracle and she would recover

*Rotjana just weeks before she died, despite incredible pain
still insisted on nursing the little ones*

*At the 100th day memorial service at Baan Than Namchai,
praying for Rotjana in front of a bronze statue of her*

THE ROAD AHEAD

For a number of years prior to her death, Rotjana had been training Game for her position at the orphanage. At twenty-eight, he is young, bright, intelligent, and like Phapet possesses a wisdom way beyond his years. He is now running Baan Than Namchai Foundation as it is now called. He is fair to every child, conscientious and honest. I do not envy him his task. He has readily accepted the responsibility to become dad to over one-hundred children, but the one thing he really has got in his favour is that he was one of them, he knows how they feel. He worries that he cannot fill Rotjana's shoes. I have had to explain to him that nobody could and no one expects him to. He must follow what is in his heart. He already is proving to be a strong but compassionate leader, and it is good to see Rotjana's staff rallying around him with support.

The foundation has become more self-sustained, the rubber plants are producing rubber to be sold, vegetables from the hydroponics unit are sold at market, and the craft shop is doing well. The future is bright, and the foundation receives tremendous support not only from ourselves but also from Willie's Orphan Fund in Northern Ireland and day-to-day running costs paid for by HATW Australia.

Phapet has just started his university course at a university in Bangkok where he is studying children's welfare because he wants to return to Baan Than Namchai to help Game.

Gon is going from strength to strength with his music, wishing to return as a music teacher and Skye no longer poops his pants, it really is just gas.

Hands Across the Water UK is no more. Shortly after Rotjana's death, I changed the name to Rotjana's Hands in memory of and out of respect to my very dear friend.

Retirement is great, we now live on our seashore here on Skye where I swim, sail, kayak and paddleboard. I am out most days with my camera as I have turned into a photography geek, spending most clear evenings out shooting aurora and the night sky.

I'm still out running most days with the dog, wild swimming with my friends around the coastline of Skye, climbing mountains and feeling so lucky to have had and still have such an amazing life.

I continue to run the charity and try to raise money however I can.

Throughout my career, I have always been blessed with good timing. Everything just slotted into place just when I needed it. I have also been blessed with having so many wonderful friends and colleagues throughout and to whom I am eternally grateful for always being there.

My amazing team: Pecky, Little Legs, Gadge, Clarky, Little Craig, Darling, Rupert and BBC who gave their all every time but sadly are no more due to financial cutbacks, my unit was closed down shortly after I retired.

The team were treated very badly by management who did not have a clue, nor did they care, and sadly this is happening more and more. When I first started my diving career, there were forty-five police dive teams in the UK; there are now fewer than ten. Whatever happened to dignity in death? Nowadays, there is very little response to deaths in water and families search the river banks themselves or pay for private diving teams to search for their loved ones. It is so sad.

This is so-called 'progress' in our modern world. I would like to think that myself and my team at least provided some dignity to the souls of the people who we never knew while living but helped them in their death.

Most importantly: thank you to my husband Ian and my mum and dad for putting up with my mad antics but never once trying to stop me. And to Rotjana for being the person you were and still are. A true angel.

Gon who is now at university studying music

*Game, an original Tsunami orphan
who is now running the home*

Enjoying life in the mountains

Swimming across the loch in front of our house

With Ian and Rhumdog celebrating Christmas

My view from the house

A publication by Plan4 Media
in association with Plan4 Publishing

Lightning Source UK Ltd.
Milton Keynes UK
UKHW020233280121
377749UK00007B/56

9 781907 463747